JUSTIN TRUDEAU ON THE ROPES

JUSTIN TRUDEAU ON THE ROPES

Governing in Troubled Times

PAUL WELLS

SQ

SUTHERLAND HOUSE

Sutherland House
416 Moore Ave., Suite 304
Toronto, ON M4G 1C9

First edition, May 2024

If you are interested in inviting one of our authors to a live event or media appearance, please contact sranasinghe@sutherlandhousebooks.com and visit our website at sutherlandhousebooks.com for more information about our authors and their schedules.

We acknowledge the support of the Government of Canada.

Manufactured in Canada
Cover designed by Shalomi Ranasinghe, and Jordan Lunn
Book composed by Karl Hunt

Library and Archives Canada Cataloguing in Publication
Title: Justin Trudeau on the ropes : governing in troubled times / Paul Wells.
Names: Wells, Paul A. (Paul Allen), author.
Description: Series statement: Sutherland quarterly ; 6
Identifiers: Canadiana (print) 20240317319 | Canadiana (ebook) 20240317408 |
ISBN 9781990823824 (softcover) | ISBN 9781990823831 (EPUB)
Subjects: LCSH: Trudeau, Justin. | LCSH: Canada—Politics and government—21st century. |
LCSH: World politics—21st century. | CSH: Canada—Politics and government—2015-
Classification: LCC FC655 .W45 2024 | DDC 971.07/4—dc23

ISBN 978-1-990823-82-4
eBook 978-1-990823-83-1

CONTENTS

In memory of Robert A. Young.

PART ONE

In March 2012, Justin Trudeau was forty-one, a freshly re-elected member of Parliament for a third-place party in the depths of despair. He was tall and confident, with piercing eyes, a magical family name, and too much time on his hands. With thirty-four MPs and a dwindling cohort of senators, the Liberal parliamentary caucus, recently shattered by the worst of three consecutive defeats at the hands of Stephen Harper's Conservatives, was the smallest it had been in Canada's history. Surely, at this moment, the Liberals needed their best talent in crucial roles. Yet the party's interim leader, Bob Rae, had appointed Trudeau his critic for youth, post-secondary education, and amateur sport. Since Parliament never debates youth, post-secondary education, or amateur sport, on most sitting days Trudeau's attendance was strictly optional.

Mostly he wandered the country giving motivational speeches and fundraising. Sometimes he'd do a charity event. At the 2010 What a Girl Wants fundraiser for the Canadian Liver Foundation at the Château Laurier hotel, Trudeau executed a saucy faux striptease—the tie was the only thing to come off—and somebody paid $1,600 for his company at lunch.

That March, the Ottawa Regional Cancer Foundation had organized an event called Fight for the Cure, at which people from the professional classes would sell tickets and box with one another awkwardly. It took Trudeau weeks to find a Conservative who would face him. Finally, a beefy, Conservative-appointed senator named Patrick Brazeau answered the call.

The two men climbed into a makeshift ring in a packed ballroom at the east-end Hampton Inn on March 31. The whole thing, ridiculously, inevitably, was broadcast live on national television. Brazeau's arms were bigger than Trudeau's legs and, in the days before the match, Brazeau's Conservative caucus colleagues had passed their time on Twitter gleefully celebrating his victory ahead of time. In the event, it took Trudeau about seven minutes to pummel Brazeau so nearly senseless that the referee stopped the fight.

Five weeks later, Trudeau's photo was on the cover of *Maclean's*, illustrating an article that said: look, maybe this guy should be the next leader of what had been, until Harper, the winningest political party in Western civilization. Forty-nine weeks after that, by God, he was. And the next time Canadians got a chance to vote on the matter, the Liberals, with Trudeau as leader, snapped a three-election losing streak and returned to power, where they remain, after a fashion, to this day.

This path to power isn't open to people of normal upbringing. If next week Jonathan Wilkinson, the bookish and detail-oriented minister of natural resources in Justin Trudeau's cabinet, decides he wants to take the next step in his political ascent, a charity boxing match will not help him. It will do Anita Anand no good to enter a pie-eating contest or for Chrystia Freeland to appear on *So You Think You Can Dance*; although, now that I mention it, I find myself wondering whether she's considered the possibility.

This is because, unlike all his predecessors and any potential successor, Trudeau has trafficked all his life in the currency of attention. Go ahead and look at him. People have been staring at him all his life. And whatever you think while you look, whether your reaction is awe or disappointment or the purest contempt, all I can tell you is, you're not the first. Somebody else had the same reaction long before you came along. Somebody else will have it after you leave. Attention is the medium through which he moves. It is his luminiferous aether.

He told an interviewer in 2002 that he was "like someone who was raised by wolves, or the person that cultivated an extremely large pumpkin." But even that didn't quite capture the strangeness of his situation, because at least the person with the pumpkin grew a pumpkin, whereas all Trudeau did was pop out of the womb. On Christmas Day, 1971, the first child of a radiant Vancouver hippie newly married to a weirdly compelling prime minister whose political honeymoon was not yet over. Which means he's not even like other political sons. There were no headlines on the day Paul Martin Jr. was born to Mr. and Mrs. Paul Martin Sr., or Preston Manning to Ernest and Muriel.

So beating up a senator wasn't an attention-getting exercise for Justin Trudeau. It was an attention-using exercise. Brazeau's face wasn't Trudeau's medium of expression: you were. Your expectations were. They still are. "Everybody is convinced that this black belt in karate with massive arms is going to clean up the pretty boy," Trudeau told a reporter before the fight, "because he grew up in the mean streets of Maniwaki and I grew up with a silver spoon in my mouth, you know? That's what everyone says, right? So, as it stands,

I can't lose. Even if I do actually lose, I know I will have gone in and people said, 'Well, there wasn't a chance anyway.'"

I begin with that stupid boxing match because apparently the damned thing is still with us even today, when the stakes for Justin Trudeau and for Canada are incomparably higher than a charity spectacle. I am told that Trudeau keeps the boxing match in his head as a reference, a model. Every time he's in trouble, he thinks, *I've been in trouble before and they were wrong to count me out.*

Of course, Trudeau is not a fool. It is as obvious to him as to you that the business of government is more important and complex than the theatre of stunts. But he likes the fight as a metaphor. He was on the ropes. Everyone was watching. Some made an early start of gloating. He won anyway. This is enough like what happened later, in the 2015 and 2019 and 2021 elections, that he mentions it sometimes to friends.

Now he is on the ropes again. The new Conservative opposition leader, Pierre Poilievre, has all but caved in Trudeau's rib cage in the opening round. To Trudeau it all feels familiar, and more reassuring than you probably expect. He has been here before, in the space between what's happening and what you expect. He knows everyone is watching. When were they not?

At the end of 2023, Trudeau met an annual appointment and gave a year-end interview to one of his oldest friends, the otherwise retired talk-radio host Terry DiMonte. When Pierre Elliott Trudeau died in 2000, Justin Trudeau hid from the crowds and the grief in Terry DiMonte's house. Now Trudeau said: "You know me well enough. You know what I believe. Do you actually think I could walk away from this fight right now?"

Again, Trudeau is no fool. He knows winners eventually lose, and a sports metaphor isn't a talisman against all ills. But if he does actually lose this time? It'll still be like Fight for the Cure, because he'll know people said there wasn't a chance anyway.

The image of Trudeau leaning against the ropes and taking his whacks is apt for another reason: because for all his pedigree and physical grace, the work of politics has never come easily for him. He is more intelligent than a lot of people are willing to believe, and at least as charming as you'd suspect, but he is no great public speaker or gifted debater. His judgment is often terrible. He has not surrounded himself with great talent; in fact, he has discovered a real gift for chasing talent away. He has announced massive reforms he had no intention of implementing, changed his mind, sometimes simply given up.

Events have buffeted him as much as any leader. Perhaps only in the last year has he begun to age in any visible way, to betray in his features and carriage even the slightest deterioration, after leading his party for a decade. But the rope-a-dope exacts its costs. Each time you pull yourself back to your feet you're less spry, your range of future action narrower.

The Liberals swept to power in 2015 after years in the wilderness, only to discover that the very manner of their ascent made them a different government from the one they had imagined, more cautious and scripted.

Trudeau fought back in 2019 from powerful self-inflicted blows— the Aga Khan vacation, the SNC-Lavalin affair, the revelation of his astonishing habit as a young man of compulsive blackfacing for social occasions. But to hang on, he had to sharply adjust his approach to campaign tactics.

Deep social divisions that were entrenched in Canada even before the COVID-19 pandemic led Trudeau to become a more starkly polarizing figure, during and since the pandemic, than he ever wanted to be.

Hard times wear leaders out. It would have been instructive to watch anyone else—a luckier Stephen Harper, say, or some imagined, more conventional Liberal—navigate the rise of Donald Trump, Brexit, a hardening of global attitudes toward China, a coarsening of discourse on social media, a deadly pandemic, a continent-wide storm of wildfires, inflation, two wars. I doubt there was any elegant way to do it. Jason Kenney's career didn't survive the times, nor Liberal governments in the two largest provinces. Assessing Trudeau requires keeping an eye on the treacherous ground he's walked.

Now he faces his most punishing test against an unsentimental bruiser named Pierre Poilievre in a moment of multiple global crises. He's come back from tough situations before, but none this tough. I offer no prediction of the outcome, but I can't look away.

* * *

If any organization in the world was ready in 2012 for a story about a plucky underdog's comeback, it was the Liberal Party of Canada. It is impossible to understand Justin Trudeau's decade as Liberal leader without studying the decade before he became its leader. It was the worst in the party's history.

The 2000 election was the party's third with Jean Chrétien as leader. The Liberals won their third consecutive majority, even healthier than in 1997, with 172 seats out of a possible 301. Chrétien was good at politics, but in an important way, winning was easier for him than for earlier or later Liberal leaders: the right-of-center vote was divided between the Progressive Conservatives and other parties, first Reform and then the Canadian Alliance. When Paul Martin became the leader at the end of 2003, that advantage vanished because the Progressive Conservatives and Canadian Alliance merged. Against Stephen Harper and a newly united Conservative Party of Canada, the Liberals were reduced to 133 seats in 2004, then again to 103 in 2006. That was the year Harper formed his first tenuous minority government.

The Liberals replaced Martin as leader with Stéphane Dion, bookish, passionate, and bereft of emotional intelligence. In the 2008 election, the Liberals were cut to seventy-seven seats. The next leader, Michael Ignatieff, somehow managed to be less appealing than Dion. In 2011, the Liberals fell to thirty-four seats. It was their lowest seat total since Confederation, and their lowest share of the popular vote—not even 19 percent.

In only a decade, the Liberals had lost half their vote and four out of every five seats they held under Chrétien. They accompanied this streak of terrible performance with a kind of self-administered vandalism, firing wave after wave of the people who had worked for each leader. Martin's staff purged Chrétien's. Dion's people fired Martin's. Ignatieff reached out to the best people he knew in Canada, but since he had spent decades at the BBC and Harvard, they were also basically the only people he knew in Canada.

These purges ransacked the Liberal party's institutional memory. Any successful political party has people on the payroll who know where the administrative offices are on Parliament Hill, or what happens to a bill after it passes second reading, or how to call in a favor. The post-Chrétien Liberals dumped all those people. In the 1940 Universal monster movie *The Mummy's Hand*, the rebel Egyptian prince, Kharis, is buried in a secret location; the slaves who buried him are killed by warriors so the secret location of his gravesite will never be known. By the early twenty-first century, the Liberal Party of Canada had adopted the plot of *The Mummy's Hand* as its human resources strategy.

In 2011, for the first time in their history, the Liberals weren't even the official Opposition in the House of Commons. Ignatieff led them to third place, behind Jack Layton's NDP. Remaining Liberal political staffers had to hand the keys to the Office of the Leader of the Opposition, or OLO, to the NDP and retreat to less prestigious digs. With perfect gallows humor, they dubbed the new office the LOL.

The ancient political journalist Peter C. Newman announced in 2009 that he had signed a contract for an insider book about Ignatieff's rise. Back then, people thought Ignatieff might rise. Instead, Newman published a 400-page political obituary, *When the Gods Changed: The Death of Liberal Canada*. Under a Harper Conservative majority government, wrote Newman, Canada would "never be the same—might even have to change its name since it will no longer be recognizable."

Trudeau was one of only two incumbent Liberal MPs in the country to win more support in 2011 than in 2008. Ignatieff lost his seat. The party would need yet another new leader. A few reporters asked Trudeau whether he was interested. Two days after the election, he told the CBC he was undecided. "The work that needs to be done is work on the ground. It's not going to be fixed by picking a cute leader or the right leader or whatever."

Five months later, in October 2011, he told CTV he'd thought it over and the answer was a firm no. "We've spent too much time talking about leadership, too much time over the past decade focused on finding that right person who is going to bring us back to the promised land as Liberals," he said. "We need to start doing the hard work on the ground."

If anything, his public comments understated Trudeau's pessimism. He told friends he was considering leaving politics. It got to a point where Bob Rae, the interim leader, organized a dinner—Rae, his wife, Arlene Perly Rae, Trudeau, and his wife, Sophie—to urge him not to quit.

Then in January 2012, the rump Liberals held their biennial policy convention in Ottawa. Days after that convention, Trudeau telephoned his old university friend, Gerald Butts, and spoke seriously for the first time about seeking the party's leadership. Exploratory meetings followed over the next nine months until Trudeau officially announced his candidacy in October.

In his memoir, you can see Trudeau struggling to reconcile his flat, public "No" with the private "Maybe" that followed on its heels. "It's more than a little ironic, but I don't think I would have run in the end had I not ruled it out so categorically several months earlier," he writes.

What changed? In his book, Trudeau attaches a lot of importance to the "unmistakable enthusiasm" of the delegates who showed up to the 2012 Ottawa convention. But partisans at a convention are always enthusiastic. Concretely, two big things changed between the 2011 drubbing and the 2012 launch of Trudeau's campaign.

First, Jack Layton died. Under the leadership of the former Toronto city councillor, the NDP gained in seats and popular vote in four consecutive elections, from 2004 to 2011. In the last of those four campaigns, the NDP surged to 103 seats, more than twice as many as they had ever won before (or since). Cancer killed Layton three months after that breakthrough. Everyone was shocked and crestfallen, a deeply felt loss.

Yet politics goes on. A week before Trudeau's boxing match against Pat Brazeau, the NDP selected as Layton's successor Thomas Mulcair, a brilliant but frosty man who had served in the provincial Liberal cabinet of Quebec premier Jean Charest. New Democrats hoped that by picking a guy in a suit who'd served in a large, centrist provincial government, they were finding someone who could close the last distance separating them from power. Of course, if Mulcair stumbled, he might open up room to the Liberals' left.

Second, the card-carrying Liberals whose enthusiasm at the Ottawa convention so impressed Trudeau passed a resolution that reduced their own influence over the party's choice of leaders.

For decades, major political parties in Canada have used their leadership contests to recruit new party members and raise money. They usually do both at the same time, by selling memberships to new members who instantly become eligible to vote on who will run the party. Leadership contests become massive membership drives. This dilutes the influence of people who've been party members for a long time, diligently coming out to debate policy or knock on doors. They get outnumbered by people who don't really know how the party functions and, having often signed up for the sole purpose of voting for their preferred leadership candidate, remain loosely attached to the party. But that's life. A few of the new members do stick around, become motivated to take part in party functions, and feed the next cycle of the party's life.

By the time Ignatieff imploded, the party's membership lists had grown so anemic that a few people were suggesting bolder measures. Why not uncouple membership growth from fundraising and make it free to vote in leadership races?

The argument in favor was that the party was close to dying. In fact, Peter C. Newman's obituary was on the bestseller lists. The Liberals needed to start showing a pulse right away; they could worry about money later. It was proposed at the Ottawa convention that the party permit a new category of "supporters" who could sign up with just their name, address, and no payment whatsoever. They would definitely be pitched later about donations, but that part was optional.

The proposal passed overwhelmingly. It made partisan affiliation easier than it had ever been for a large Canadian political party, at the price of making it less meaningful than ever. Trudeau was a big supporter of the measure. I ran into him in a hallway at the Westin Ottawa, next to the convention venue, on Friday night as delegates were wandering from one suite party to the next. He told me that with mass email becoming the communications tool of choice for political parties, it was more important to have those contacts than to have a little money from each.

While we were talking, a cheerfully inebriated young Liberal spotted Trudeau and wandered up to chat. Trudeau turned from me to the party guy and told him, in a quiet voice with an edge,

"I'm talking here. I'll get to you in a minute." All the light went out of the party guy's face. He beat a hasty retreat. It was a reminder that Trudeau has spent his life both stoking and dampening the enthusiasm of strangers.

The other big advantage of the "supporter" class was that it gave a huge advantage to leadership candidates with big name recognition, because a lot of supporters would do no further research into the party's rules and personalities. It was now even more pointless to run against a Trudeau.

Marc Garneau was appalled to learn this lesson. Garneau was the first Canadian in space, a veteran of three NASA space shuttle missions, and a career naval officer before that. He had schools named after him. As recently as 2008, Stéphane Dion had refused to let Trudeau run in the safe seat of Westmount because he wanted to reserve Westmount for Garneau. To Dion, Garneau seemed a surer value for the party than Trudeau. But, in 2012, in the eyes of a sea of Johnny-come-lately "supporters," Garneau's name might as well have been Bleep Blorp. He dropped out weeks before voting began.

In April 2013, Trudeau won 80 percent of the votes cast in the first round. There remained only the question of what he wanted the Liberal party to stand for.

During the leadership campaign, he had said nothing to make this question easy to answer. "We will have a very detailed platform in 2015," he told Global News during the campaign. "But between now and then, it is not up to, you know, a leader or leadership candidate and a tight group of people to find out all the answers. It is about us engaging with Canadians right across the country to develop these solutions."

In private, even Trudeau's "tight group of people" had a hundred different ideas about where Trudeau might take the party. The summer before his leadership bid, as the last stage before Trudeau and Sophie finally committed to entering the race, his advisors, Gerald Butts and Katie Telford, organized a three-day weekend retreat at Mont Tremblant, northwest of Montreal. A few dozen people came out, including Trudeau's brother, Sacha, and some future cabinet ministers, Navdeep Bains and Omar Alghabra.

In his memoir, Trudeau describes the group's opening conversation around a campfire. The question he put to his embryonic brain trust was simple enough: why did you come here? "People talked about economic opportunity and education, natural resources and climate change, immigration and diversity," he writes. "My Papineau riding president . . . said that he thought Canada was becoming a much less fair country under the Conservatives. Several Quebecers in the group expressed deep regret that their province had lost its voice." A guy from British Columbia talked about "putting that dynamic part of Canada at the heart of our political movement."

When it was Trudeau's turn to explain why he was there, "I concluded very simply that I believed this country was better than its current government. Canadians are broad minded and big-hearted, fair and honest, hard-working, hopeful, and kind. I said Canada had some big issues to tackle, but none bigger than those we had successfully wrestled in the past. I told people that for me, the greatest of all this country's many blessings is our diversity, and that this meant the people who lead Canada need to be open-minded and generous of spirit toward all, not just toward those who agree with them and support them."

To Trudeau, the "basic flaw" in Stephen Harper's government was "its inability to relate to or work with people who do not share its ideological predisposition. . . . In short, I said that I was there because the government needed to be replaced."

It doesn't do to be cynical about these things. We are all better off if people who want to lead the country brainstorm and dream with other people before committing. The optimism of Canadians who want to lead will always be rare and valuable. That being said, one sifts through Trudeau's account in vain for anything surprising or insightful.

It would actually have been difficult to gather any supporters around any candidate for the leadership of any major party over the last thirty years without somebody saying a kind word for opportunity, education, and a strong voice for Quebec and the West. Most would also have something nice to say about diversity and the fight against climate change. As for the rationale Trudeau offered when his turn came—to replace the government—it imposed a mandate that would be fulfilled the day after an election victory. If you're there because "the government needs replacing," your work is done once you replace it.

Of course, this was only the first conversation of many at that Tremblant weekend. Trudeau offers a hint of what came later. Some of the conversation was "pretty technical," he writes. "I'll spare you having to indulge my inner geek by not running on about data, GOTV (get out the vote) techniques, small-gift fundraising, and the fine points of our social media strategy." This is a reminder that Trudeau has never been motivated only by principles so broad as to sound like platitudes. He is also, by all accounts, a keen student of the riding-level mechanics of voter identification and motivation. It's something he shares with his childhood friend, Tom Pitfield, who was his chief digital strategist for the leadership and for every national campaign since. This fascination with squeezing the largest number of seats out of a given share of the popular vote would come in handy in 2019 and 2021, when Trudeau's Liberals held onto power with the smallest shares of the popular vote of any government in Canada's history.

Data and GOTV are also worth keeping in mind because political journalism tends to focus too closely on what leaders say. The ground game—email solicitation and face-to-face interactions at the door, using voter-tracking software to put limited resources where they'll help the most—is often crucial and rarely makes headlines.

The participants at the Tremblant weekend persuaded one another that a Trudeau candidacy could work. After Trudeau won the leadership, the Liberals shot from third place in polls to first, where they would remain for a year and a half. The Conservatives didn't even wait until Trudeau had been the leader for a week before launching a barrage of mocking TV ads, drawn from the ample stockpile of archival footage of Trudeau wearing his hair long and saying funny things. This was straight out of the Harper playbook that had laid Dion and Ignatieff low. But this time the ads had no perceptible effect.

When the Trudeau Liberals' lead finally frayed at the end of 2014, it probably had less to do with Conservative ads than with the unflattering contrast between the leaders' performance in the House of Commons. Harper was in hot water over the revelation that his chief of staff had written a personal cheque to cover the travel expenses of Senator Mike Duffy. It was the kind of juicy procedural mess the NDP's Mulcair loved. He used Question Period to press Harper mercilessly and with real prosecutorial skill. Harper seemed energized by the challenge, and gave almost as good as he got. Stuck leading the third party, Trudeau got only a sliver of the available time in the Commons and rarely had anything useful to add. It wasn't clear why he needed a seat in Parliament, let alone lead a government there.

By spring of the election year 2015, Trudeau's long lead in the polls had ended and the Liberals were back in third place. The image of the fighter on the ropes was now appropriate. Liberals in Ottawa were starting to tell themselves that beating Harper might take two elections, which was awkward for the new leader: the party had ejected Dion and Ignatieff after a single defeat each. Trudeau couldn't rely on a second chance. Indeed, the party itself couldn't. If the Liberals landed behind the NDP again, the party's survival might well be at risk.

Trudeau didn't sweat the pressure. I had a chance to observe him on Saturday, May 2. The US ambassador to Ottawa in those days was a Chicago banker named Bruce Heyman. Heyman's wife, Vicki, was from Kentucky, and they liked to hold a reception at their official residence in swank Rockcliffe Park to watch the Kentucky Derby on television. Assorted figures from the Ottawa social set came out to watch the two-minute horse race after sitting through the interminable preliminaries. The bar was stocked with bourbon for mint juleps. Ladies wore fancy hats and bright dresses, men whatever they could find in an Ottawa closet that might resemble seersucker.

Trudeau was there with Sophie and her parents. I didn't take photos, but his outfit was faintly ridiculous: white shoes, light jacket, some kind of Panama hat at a rakish angle, no socks. I chatted awkwardly with him for a few minutes in one of the residence's ground-floor rooms. I said I was never good at dress-up parties. It had been hard enough for me to learn how to dress like a grown-up, I said, so I stuck to that. Trudeau smirked: "I gave up on trying to do that a long time ago."

I mentioned an event the Liberals had announced for the week ahead, to unveil a new social policy for the election. There would be more of these events as the year went on, Trudeau confirmed. "Harper and the pundits say we have no ideas," he said. "It's going to be so easy to disprove that."

Two days later, at a family-style restaurant in Aylmer, Quebec, a short drive from Ottawa, Trudeau announced the first elements of his economic platform. A Liberal government would increase taxes on incomes over $200,000 from 29 percent to 33 percent. Taxes on lower incomes would be cut. For most parents of young children, the Liberals would replace Harper's taxable Universal Child Care Benefit with a bigger, tax-free Canada Child Benefit that wouldn't be available to higher-income parents. "We can do more for the people who need it by doing less for the people who don't," Trudeau said.

Later, after they won the election, the Liberals' polls showed that three of their most popular platform planks were the ones Trudeau announced on that May morning in Aylmer. Increasing taxes on the highest incomes was the most popular. Reducing taxes on lower incomes came next. The enhanced child benefit was third. In fourth place was something Trudeau announced later: support for Ontario

Liberal premier Kathleen Wynne's plan to enhance Canada Pension Plan benefits by increasing mandatory contributions.

These four policies had a common theme. They were broad economic policies that were designed to make life more affordable for most Canadians. Together, they positioned Trudeau perceptibly to Harper's left, but not very far. They represented the mildest form of middle-class populism.

The close Trudeau associate who told me of these poll results said, years later, "We were never going to convince anyone that Justin Trudeau was just like them. But we tried really hard to persuade them that this silver-spoon celebrity would find ways to make Ottawa work better for ordinary people like them."

Looking through my records, I'm reminded that there was another reason why my Kentucky Derby chat with Trudeau was tense. My employers at *Maclean's* had already sent him an invitation to take part in a nationally televised leaders' debate, with me as moderator. I didn't raise the matter with Trudeau. It was a sensitive subject for him. Of the four leaders who ended up participating, he would be the last to accept the invitation. He saw it as a kind of trap. He wasn't entirely wrong.

The debate was happening because Harper didn't want to cooperate with the consortium of broadcast networks that had organized every English-language election debate since the first in 1968. He didn't trust the overstuffed consortium debates with their long lines of TV star moderators and their pre-taped questions from "ordinary Canadians" selected by some news producer in Toronto. But Harper didn't want to avoid debates altogether. In fact, for this campaign more than any other, he preferred multiple debates. In this, he had company. Mulcair also wanted a campaign in which all the party leaders did a lot of talking. Harper and Mulcair considered themselves champion talkers. They were less impressed with Trudeau.

Brian Mulroney had told an interviewer that Mulcair was "probably the best Opposition leader since John Diefenbaker." Nobody had comparable praise for Trudeau. The Conservatives and New Democrats figured that if more people could watch a version of the same lopsided debating dynamic, again and again, Trudeau's goose would be cooked. Harper, Mulcair, and their campaign staffs put the word out that they would entertain independent proposals for leaders' debates. *Maclean's* bit right away, followed by the organizers of Toronto's Munk Debates and the *Globe and Mail*.

Trudeau had been training for a very specific kind of debate: the stately broadcast-consortium format that Harper and Mulcair had torpedoed. He didn't like all these weird, off-brand contests. He dithered for days after the other leaders had accepted the assorted invitations. Finally, he agreed to show up.

We gathered August 6 in a ground-floor studio in the CityTV building at Yonge-Dundas Square in Toronto. Our Rogers corporate partners at CityTV never liked the debate project, which they saw as a dumb reason to throw away a night's ad revenue. On one of our early conference calls, I said something about the target audience for the event. "Who's our audience for a debate in August?" a CityTV executive shot back. "Fucking nobody."

A debate is a strange thing.

Before the cameras came on, Harper, Mulcair, Trudeau, and Green Party leader Elizabeth May were surprisingly cordial with one another. Practitioners of the same craft, they milled awkwardly and made small talk.

Eventually, showtime approached and the leaders took their places behind white lecterns. Each stand held a microphone and a flat surface for the leader's prepared notes. Further down, out of view of the camera, was a little shelf tucked inside the lectern's casing, just big enough to hold a glass of water. Harper must have whacked his with a knee. There was a muted crash. A puddle spread on the floor around Harper. With barely a minute to go before the debate went live, the Conservative leader looked stricken and helpless. Was he supposed to get down on his knees and risk going on air butt-up, trying to scoop water up with his bare hands? Was he supposed to just stand there in the center of a growing puddle and try to look prime ministerial?

The crisis lasted only a few seconds. A CityTV floor director hopped forward to mop up the water, retreating from the shot just as the debate began. Nobody at home was the wiser. But Trudeau told friends later that, for just a few seconds, Harper had stood there walleyed, with no idea how to respond. In a competitive setting, few things brighten spirits more than the sight of an opponent's discomfort. If Harper was capable of running into a little shitty luck, Trudeau said, that must mean he was human and hence not invulnerable. "If it bleeds," Arnold Schwarzenegger said in the 1987 film *Predator*, "we can kill it."

Far from burying Trudeau, the *Maclean's* debate was the moment he came off the ropes. Of the ten most recent public-opinion polls before the debate, five had shown Mulcair's NDP in the lead, two had the Harper Conservatives leading, and three showed the two parties in a tie. After the debate, the Conservatives began a long, slow fall in the polls that lasted for the rest of August, matched by a slow but steady climb out of the basement by the third-place Liberals. For most of September, the three parties were roughly tied, with no clear leader among them. In the campaign's final days, Trudeau's Liberals began to pull ahead. The Liberals finished seven points ahead of the Conservatives and twenty points ahead of the NDP. The two older leaders had hatched an innovative plan to corner Trudeau in a series of national debates and talk him into early retirement. Their plan failed.

In hindsight, what's most striking about 2015 is the story Trudeau told, in the debates and throughout his campaign, about the government he hoped to lead. He invited voters to imagine a moderate government focused on the economy and on Canada's traditional advantages, including resource exports.

"Is Stephen Harper's plan working for you?" he asked in the first two minutes of the *Maclean's* debate. "He took a decade of surpluses and turned it into eight consecutive deficits."

Trudeau was also the last leader to speak in that debate. As he would throughout the campaign, he emphasized the unifying power of economic growth. "An economy that works for the middle class means a country that works for everyone, a country that is strong not in spite of our differences but because of them."

The word "carbon" was pronounced nineteen times in the two-hour debate. Elizabeth May, the Green Party leader, used the word four times. Harper used it six times, Mulcair once, and as the moderator, I used the word "carbon" seven times. Trudeau said "carbon" only once, to depict the federal government's job as nearly finished. "Eighty-six percent of our economy have committed to put a price on carbon"—ding ding ding!—"with the actions of four different provinces that have taken up the leadership that [Harper's] government has simply not shown," he said. In other words: thanks to Liberal provincial governments in Quebec, Ontario, and British Columbia, and Rachel Notley's new NDP government in Alberta, almost all the hard work was done. "The Liberal party is focused on working with those provinces to make sure we do reduce emissions," Trudeau said, "because that's what, actually, Canadians expect in order to be good players in the global economy."

At the *Globe and Mail* debate six weeks later, the moderator asked Trudeau how he could claim to have a national plan if the provinces did all the work. Trudeau retorted that this was the only way it could work. "The idea of imposing a bureaucracy out of Ottawa . . . on provinces like British Columbia, that have already moved forward with a world-renowned carbon tax that is actually working for them, is actually a completely nonsensical plan."

Debates are chaotic, of course. For anyone who wanted Trudeau's plan in detail, there was the printed platform. But even in print, he came across as a guy who didn't want to talk much about climate.

The term "middle class" appeared 133 times in Trudeau's 2015 election platform, including in its title. The word "climate" didn't appear until page thirteen, to set up a promise of "significant new investments in green infrastructure." The word "carbon" appeared only ten times. Six of those mentions referred to a "Low Carbon Economy Trust," a plan to give provinces money to reward them for developing policies that cut carbon emissions, like energy retrofit programs for houses. The other four mentions of carbon were passing references to a price on carbon that would be easily agreed with cooperative provinces. A Trudeau government would "ensure that the provinces and territories have targeted federal funding and the flexibility to design their own policies to meet these commitments, including their own carbon pricing policies," the platform said.

Trudeau's first majority government, his only one to date, was not a historic sweep. He didn't run the table the way Mulroney did in 1984 or Diefenbaker in 1958. But the really big majorities are just a headache, anyway. This one would do.

"Over the past three years, you told us what you're going through," he told supporters in his victory speech. "You told us that it's getting harder and harder to make ends meet, let alone to get ahead. You told us you're worried about whether you'll be able to afford a dignified retirement. You told us that your communities need investment. You told us you need a fair shot at better jobs. You are the inspiration for our efforts. You are the reason why we worked so hard to be here tonight, and you will be at the heart of this new government."

PART TWO

The troubles of the world seemed far distant on the lovely, early November day when Trudeau, Sophie, and the telegenic members of the new cabinet strolled up the driveway of Rideau Hall so the government could take the oaths of office.

Almost all of them needed to take three oaths each. If you've never been a member of a federal cabinet, you first have to swear allegiance to the Crown. In 2015, that still meant the Queen. Then you must take a separate oath as a member of the Privy Council. That one is my favorite: "Generally, in all things I shall do as a faithful and true servant ought to do for Her Majesty," as it said then, or "His Majesty" now.

Only after you've taken the first two oaths can you take the oath that's specific to your new portfolio. The first two oaths don't wear off over time, so returning ministers with previous cabinet experience need only take the third oath. Very few of Trudeau's ministers had been in cabinet before. He sure hadn't.

The decade-long collapse of the old Liberal party would keep imposing its costs even after Trudeau returned the party to power. Since 80 percent of the seats the Liberals held in 2000 were lost to other parties by 2011, winning them back meant that 80 percent of the new governing caucus were rookie MPs.

It is normal and healthy to have around a cabinet table people who've never held a ministerial portfolio before. It is rarer to have multiple ministers in senior roles who've never even been Members of Parliament, who don't yet know where the bathrooms are or which direction to face during Question Period. And yet here they were: Bill Morneau in Finance, Jane Philpott at Health, Jody Wilson-Raybould at Justice, Harjit Sajjan at Defence. Chrystia Freeland, Jim Carr, Catherine McKenna, Hunter Tootoo, Mélanie Joly, Kent Hehr, Amarjeet Sohi, Maryam Monsef. Most of them didn't even know most of the others. It was like their first day at sleep-away camp.

After they took their oaths, they walked outside Rideau Hall and stood in rows on risers behind Trudeau so they would be in the camera frame as he took his first questions from reporters as Canada's new prime minister. Why were half of the ministers women? "Because it's 2015," Trudeau said. The line captured the mood of an era. News of it would travel around the world within minutes.

But from that first day, there was a structural tension built into his government. Who was in charge, and to what degree? Stephen Harper, in the popular imagination, had governed as a recluse. Trudeau said he would do the opposite. "This is going to be a period of slight adjustment in the political world in Canada, because government by cabinet is back," he said. Behind him, his smiling ministers, arranged in ranks, nodded enthusiastically.

Well, wait a minute. Were they the team he described, or the backdrop they resembled? Were they there to engage in a clash of ideas, or to nod and smile?

It soon became clear that Trudeau preferred harmony to internal debate. The party he inherited had been divided into factions since before he was born. He would have none of that. But that preference had the cost that groupthink always does: a deafness to internal dissent even when it had a point; a conformity of viewpoint, enforced through social norms more than with formal rules; and, over time, the steady departure of people who fell from Trudeau's favor, or he from theirs.

Trudeau's aides knew the cabinet was a green cabinet, but it wasn't as though there were more experienced ministerial candidates waiting in the wings. They had to hope for the best. A lot of the new ministers had impressive real-world experience, in business or academia or the public sector. Some of that experience would inform their new work. The new ministers would have plenty of help from their staffs, although, again, given the waves of purges under previous doomed Liberal leaders, most of the staffers were new to governing too. The rookies faced learning curves. In theory, that should front-load most of the hard work and embarrassment. Each day should run more smoothly than the last. In theory.

All these rookies in senior cabinet roles presented a management problem for Trudeau's PMO. Under the guidance of Katie Telford, a former Ontario provincial government staffer who has been Trudeau's chief of staff for all of his time in office, the cabinet was well supervised. It spent a lot of time on team-building exercises. The ministers spent more time together than cabinets usually do, often on weekend retreats outside of Ottawa. They were invited to brainstorm while someone took notes on a whiteboard. Each could count on the advice of his or her own chief of staff, a Liberal partisan who ran the minister's office and helped the minister navigate the unfamiliar Ottawa corridors. Ministers' chiefs of staff were appointed by Trudeau's own staff—chiefly Telford and Gerald Butts, Trudeau's principal secretary and McGill University classmate—sometimes over the objections of the ministers for whom they worked.

Bill Morneau hoped his chief would be a guy named John Zerucelli. Zerucelli had worked in Jean Chrétien's PMO as a young man and gone on to senior roles in Ontario's Liberal governments and at a bunch of big companies. Butts told Morneau his chief would be Richard Maksymetz, a longtime federal Liberal organizer who had attended the Mont Tremblant campout that launched Trudeau's leadership campaign. "I could not help wondering about the PMO's unbending insistence on Richard filling the position," Morneau wrote in his memoir.

He wasn't the only one. "Without even talking to me, Gerry and Katie had determined who my first chief of staff would be before I was even sworn in," Wilson-Raybould wrote in her memoir. "Ultimately, on a phone call after some back and forth, Gerry said 'trust me'; he added that I needed to 'take a leap of faith.'" It didn't work out. Wilson-Raybould's chosen minder lasted only two months. Even later on, she wrote, "the PMO insisted that no ministers meet with each other unless their chiefs of staff were present." This is an astonishing requirement. It amounts to a rule that private conversations among competent adults could not take place if the adults in question were cabinet colleagues.

Some new ministers also chafed at the heavy fundraising requirements associated with their roles. Ministers were expected to show up regularly at Liberal party fundraisers, where their presence would attract new donors and make those who'd already given feel special. Ministers' senior staffers were expected to donate the annual maximum allowed by law: $1,500 at the time.

Trudeau set the example for enthusiastic fundraising. The *Globe and Mail* reported that Trudeau showed up at the opulent Vancouver home of a Chinese-Canadian business executive in May for a $1,500-a-head fundraiser. Weeks later, one of the guests, Zhang Bin, donated $200,000 to the Pierre Elliott Trudeau Foundation in Montreal. It's never been clear what Zhang hoped to accomplish with the gift, although "furthering the important work of the Pierre Elliott Trudeau Foundation" somehow isn't the first explanation that comes to mind.

While they were adjusting to the burden of fundraising and working with PMO-appointed senior staff, cabinet ministers also learned that the boss's patience for freewheeling debate was sharply limited. Naysayers soon developed bad reputations. Scott Brison, whose job as Treasury Board president was to make sure money would only be spent on things that worked and were useful, was seen as a downer. One chief of staff told me Brison sounded like the schoolteacher in the old *Peanuts* cartoons, a trombone with a wah-wah mute. After twenty-two years in the House of Commons and barely three in cabinet, he would quit in 2019. Jane Philpott and Jody Wilson-Raybould were sometimes called "the mean girls" for their willingness to criticize colleagues' work. In 2017, Stéphane Dion and John McCallum, two of the oldest men in cabinet, were told they were suddenly needed in diplomatic posts thousands of miles away. Later, after the 2021 election, Trudeau told Marc Garneau he wasn't needed in cabinet at all.

The no-griping rules applied to staff as well as ministers. Cyrus Reporter, a lawyer and lifelong Liberal who was Trudeau's chief of staff until the 2015 election, often gave vent to a pessimism he had earned through long service in the Chrétien government. For this he was nicknamed "the disapproving uncle." He soon went back to the private sector.

Tension and turnover are common features of any large organization. Most people everywhere set their personal preferences aside for the success of a larger organization. The Trudeau government posted significant early wins. The new government passed its most popular measures in short order: the enhanced child benefit, the higher taxes on richer folks, the lower taxes for everyone else, the pay-more-to-get-more pension reform. These weren't cosmetic changes. Statistics Canada found the number of children living in households below the poverty line fell by 278,000 between 2015 and 2017.

The Liberals brought energy and a basic affability to their other tasks. An ambassador from Europe told me that, for the first time since he had arrived in Ottawa during the late Harper years, he was actually getting calls returned from members of the government who were eager to help: "It's as though Harry Potter has replaced Voldemort!" In due time, the government legalized cannabis, sharply increased spending in Indigenous communities, and signed the Paris agreement on reducing carbon emissions. There was plenty of activity.

Over time, however, the team showed signs of wear and tear. Brison's departure forced a cabinet shuffle, which Trudeau used to deal with Jody Wilson-Raybould. She had spent the fall of 2018 making herself a particularly vexing example of government by cabinet.

Quebec's giant SNC-Lavalin engineering firm had been charged in 2015 with fraud and bribery related to millions of dollars in payments to public officials in Libya. A year later, the firm started lobbying for legislation that would introduce a novel form of out-of-court settlement, a so-called "deferred prosecution agreement," into Canadian law. In 2018, that lobbying effort paid off. It fell to the director of public prosecutions, Kathleen Roussel, to decide whether SNC-Lavalin qualified for a deferred prosecution agreement. She decided it didn't because, as she told the *Globe*'s Robert Fife much later, the charges facing SNC-Lavalin suggested behavior that was egregious and longstanding. That left to Wilson-Raybould the decision of whether to overrule Roussel. If she did, she would become the first attorney general to countermand any director of public prosecutions. She decided not to. In later testimony to a parliamentary committee, she suggested it wasn't even a hard call.

The most astonishing circus ensued. In over a dozen meetings across three months, a procession of Wilson-Raybould's supposed political colleagues—Trudeau, Butts, Telford, other PMO staffers, Bill Morneau as finance minister, and Michael Wernick as clerk of the Privy Council—met to ask her if she wouldn't reconsider. And when, after all that time, she still hadn't changed her mind about what seems to have been an open-and-shut decision, Trudeau removed her from her post. Trudeau busted Wilson-Raybould down to veterans' affairs minister in the post-Brison shuffle. The details of his office's pressure campaign against her found their way into the *Globe*, then into testimony at a Commons committee. The political crisis that followed was the worst of Trudeau's career.

Why did an obscure dispute over the prerogatives of the attorney general hurt so much? A lot of reasons. First, because it suggested—hell, it *demonstrated*—that there were two Trudeau governments. One for the rest of us—pot shops on every corner!—and another for giant corporations that could afford the finest lobbyists. SNC-Lavalin wanted fundamental rules of the legal system changed in mid-course, after it was already facing charges, over the objections of the government's chief prosecutor and the minister in charge of the justice system. Trudeau moved heaven and earth to deliver and, when he got caught, his first instinct was to deny everything.

Second, Wilson-Raybould was subjected to something that a lot of people were feeling at this point: the Trudeau government as an elaborate ritual of enforced conformity. Precisely because he knew he wasn't supposed to put pressure on an attorney general in the exercise of her functions, Trudeau sent a succession of emissaries to just sort of . . . check in on her. To ask how she was doing. Wilson-Raybould was asked, dozens of times by many different people, whether she was sure about her decision. Nobody ever took her "my decision is final" as final.

A few words could apply to this spectacle. "Gaslighting" comes to mind. But as much as anything, it was peer pressure. Trudeau sent the team to ask what her decision was, but the point of sending the team was to make sure she knew what the decision was. I think that he and his team were astonished that she declined to take the repeated hint. Wilson-Raybould honestly believed "government by cabinet" gave her not just a right to disagree with the PMO, but an obligation to stick to her guns in defense of an important principle. Soon enough, she was gone.

The message to the surviving ministers was clear: you are free to disagree, right up until we ask if you mean it. Then, by God, fall in. Forever after, when people outside the government wondered why nobody spoke up against one boneheaded scheme or another, people inside knew that speaking up meant putting your career on the line.

Eventually, it wouldn't be enough for Trudeau that his ministers think like him. Soon, he would expect the rest of us to do the same.

* * *

As the Trudeau team struggled with growing pains, its plan became more of a burden than a resource. Ten months after the 2015 election, someone who helped write the 2015 Liberal platform told me it was at least a third too long. Politics imposes harsh limits on any government. There are only so many hours in a day, so many Parliamentary sitting days in a year. The government was always under a deadline. The Liberals actually accomplished a lot. But their glut of glib promises soon led to gridlock. The promises they failed to deliver would end up hurting.

At Immigration, John McCallum set up a nearly round-the-clock operation to get 25,000 Syrian refugees accepted through government sponsorship by the end of 2015. A special cabinet committee led by Jane Philpott ensured McCallum of support across the government. In the end, the government missed its self-imposed end-of-year deadline by two months, but it still left the impression this new government could get big things done well.

The Supreme Court ruled in 2015 that the government had until June 2016 to give gravely ill patients the option of medically assisted death. Philpott and Wilson-Raybould bonded over the work of drawing up the new legislation. Their bill passed into law on time, although the top court would find it unreasonably narrow in scope, forcing amendments three years later.

Meanwhile, the Supremes had left the new government another deadline: to rejig the RCMP's labor-relations regime. No government in history has ever been in a rush to fix the RCMP. As these bills crowded more exciting elements of the Trudeau agenda off the Commons order paper, Trudeau let his impatience show in two ways.

First, he had his House leader, Dominic LeBlanc, introduce a motion to give the government new powers for rushing bills through debate. If implemented, the motion would have allowed the government to force overnight debates, adjourn the House without notice, and limit the opposition parties' attempts to slow things down. This was the opposite of the freewheeling, open-ended debate Trudeau campaigned on. But every opposition politician loves debate as much as every governing politician mistrusts it. Trudeau had made the transition. He now believed debate could only slow his work down, not improve it.

LeBlanc's motion was the formal expression of Trudeau's mounting frustration. Its informal expression was more startling. One day on the House of Commons floor, during debate on the assisted-dying bill, Mulcair and some NDP MPs physically blocked Gord Brown, the Conservative whip, from engaging in a bit of traditional parliamentary ceremony. The people's business couldn't proceed while the New Democrats blocked Brown's path. It was ridiculous, but what could anyone do about it? Trudeau knew. We bring old skills to each new workplace, and he used to be a nightclub bouncer. He strode across the aisle, shouted at the New Democrats to "Get the fuck out of my way," and grabbed Brown by the arm. Trudeau's elbow landed in the chest of an NDP MP, Ruth Ellen Brosseau.

So much for any hope of speeding things up. The Commons spent five hours the next day debating Trudeau's outburst. He wore himself hoarse, apologizing. LeBlanc withdrew the motion that would have given him sweeping powers to limit debate. But that simply meant debates would keep crawling along at their traditional pace. Trudeau learned to stop inflicting body checks on fellow parliamentarians, but he never got over his disdain for the pokey, unglamorous routines of the House of Commons.

Slowly, the sum of all the new government's triumphs, defeats, and compromises started to move it quite far from the modest, centrist Liberalism Trudeau peddled in the 2015 election. It took Morneau a month to admit it, but his tax increases on affluent Canadians would never pay for his tax cuts on lower incomes. It took longer to admit that Trudeau's promise of a balanced budget after only two years of deficits was built on smoke. Deficit spending became chronic.

As for Trudeau's faith that his environmental credentials would actually help him get more of Alberta's oil to market: that one died many deaths. Only days after the Trudeau government was sworn in, Barack Obama said he wouldn't change his mind and permit the Keystone XL pipeline into the United States. In 2017, TransCanada abandoned its Energy East pipeline project. Trudeau blamed the low price of crude, but that's not what TransCanada told the National Energy Board. The company blamed the "existing and likely future delays resulting from the regulatory process." A year later, Kinder Morgan put its westward-facing Trans Mountain pipeline expansion on hold. Trudeau took the astonishing step of buying the damned pipeline, at an initial cost of $4.5 billion, to ensure its completion. That bill would balloon sevenfold over the next six years.

Trudeau campaigned on the premise that the only necessary ingredient for Canada's success as an energy exporter was Stephen Harper's forced retirement. He believed environmental virtue could go hand in hand with increased energy exports. Now it seemed he couldn't deliver either.

Provinces were increasingly disinclined to do the heavy lifting on carbon pricing. Liberal or Liberal-friendly governments went down to defeat in Quebec, Ontario, Alberta, and most of the Atlantic provinces. Before that happened, at the end of 2016, premiers signed an agreement with Trudeau that looked great at the time. It said Ottawa would impose a carbon tax in provinces that refused, and "return revenues to the jurisdiction of origin."

Now there were a lot of provinces refusing. Trudeau realized he'd promised to send carbon-tax revenues to the recalcitrant new Conservative provincial governments. In effect, he was on the record as promising cash windfalls to the governments that liked him least. He quickly came up with a better idea: send the money to individuals instead. The resulting "rebate" would limit or even exceed the cost of paying the tax for most individuals. In the early going, the rebate plan gave Trudeau a useful rebuttal against an emerging common front of provincial premiers who opposed his carbon tax.

Keeping his climate promises has been harder than Trudeau had ever imagined, but he has never stopped working on them. Another major campaign promise simply went out the window. Trudeau had said that the 2015 election would be Canada's last under the first-past-the-post system that had returned Harper's only majority government. It was a great way to turn voter fatigue with Harper into fuel for the Liberals. It worked even better because he didn't say which new system he'd introduce. There are two main alternatives to first-past-the-post: proportional representation, which would tend to dilute the Liberal party's influence; and ranked balloting, which would tend to enhance it. There was no way to do both. As 2016 wore on, public opinion consolidated behind proportional representation. In 2017, Trudeau sent his new electoral-reform minister, Karina Gould, to announce there would be no reform at all.

In Yellowknife a week later, Trudeau depicted his transparent con as the highest virtue. If he'd introduced a change to the voting system "that would augment individual voices, that would augment extremist voices and activist voices . . . I think we'd be entering an era of instability and uncertainty," he said. "We'd be putting at risk the very thing that makes us luckier than anyone else on the planet: the fact that we look at our differences as something to draw on and discover and build on, as opposed to emphasize and highlight."

All of this was less incomprehensible than it might have been, because, by the beginning of 2017, voters understood the context: the world had become a place where "extremist voices" were getting louder. Notwithstanding his comments on electoral reform, Trudeau would respond to this new world by adjusting his politics to more effectively emphasize and highlight the difference.

External events were something else—beyond his team being inexperienced and his plan overstuffed—that undermined the performance of Justin Trudeau's government. He couldn't give his government's problems nearly enough attention because the rest of the world was in turmoil, usually in ways Canada was powerless to fix.

Trudeau had such high hopes for the world and Canada's place in it when he was elected. In February 2016, he threw a dinner for

Ban Ki-Moon, the secretary general of the United Nations, at the sprawling Canadian Museum of History in Gatineau. Hundreds of guests were there, including every living former Liberal foreign minister and one former Conservative foreign minister, Joe Clark. Ban repeated a bit of post-election Liberal rhetoric, telling the crowd that "Canada is back!" Nobody could blame him. He was in a good mood. Trudeau had told him Canada would contribute more troops to UN peacekeeping operations and compete for a rotating non-permanent seat on the UN Security Council.

In fact, the peacekeeping contribution wouldn't begin for two more years and would be so small as to be negligible. After a mission to Mali ended in 2019, Canada had fewer peacekeepers deployed overseas than at any point since modern peacekeeping began in 1956. The Security Council bid lost by even more votes than Canada's previous candidacy under Harper. It was a cold shoulder for Trudeau's Canada.

Of course, the cordial divorce between Trudeau and his dreams of a better world wasn't all about Trudeau. The world was going through some stuff. Canada would be lucky just to hang on.

In March 2016, a month after Ban Ki-Moon's Ottawa visit, Trudeau took nine cabinet ministers and a planeload of journalists to Washington for a two-day visit with Barack Obama. There was a party when the delegation arrived in Washington. The Weeknd, a medium-high-profile Canadian pop star, dropped by. The PMO sent out lists of the fashion designers whose clothes Sophie was wearing. And, yes, there was a state dinner and some serious work aligning the agendas of two governments. It felt like the launch of a new era. But Obama's presidency was in its last year and everyone was trying to take the measure of a troubling new development in US politics.

On the flight home from Washington, Trudeau told reporters he was watching Donald Trump's candidacy for the Republican nomination with interest. "You could argue that I won because I read the public better than the other leaders did," Trudeau said. "I think Trump might be the guy down here with the best read of American voters." It was a good call.

Yet Trump represented a rejection of most of the things Trudeau was trying to do at home and in the world. He was against free-trade agreements, multilateralism, immigration, NATO—the whole apparatus the Trudeau team embraced with the catch-all term "rules-based international order."

The first sign that the old, optimistic political consensus was under siege came in June, when Britain voted to leave the European Union. Trump's election in November was much more of the same, and far more threatening to Canada. It was a political earthquake.

During his campaign against Hillary Clinton, Trump had called the continental NAFTA free-trade zone "the worst trade deal" the US had ever made. Taking the measure of this erratic new president, and trying to counter his instinct to blow up every trading relationship the US had, became full-time work for Trudeau's government. Two months after the presidential election, Trudeau shuffled his cabinet, replacing Stéphane Dion with Chrystia Freeland in the global-affairs portfolio. Freeland was a regular on CNN talk shows during her days as a journalist. She had better connections in Washington than anyone else in Trudeau's government.

Trudeau was determined to charm the new guy as much as possible. "We're Canadians," he'd told his stunned advisors on election night. "We can get along with anyone." Telford and Butts made frequent trips to Washington to make nice with such Trump advisors as Jared Kushner, Steve Bannon, Peter Navarro, and others. But what enabled the Canadians to get the main elements of NAFTA carried forward into a new deal was a basic insight: they understood the stakes were so high that they couldn't depend on a few personal relationships at the top.

One of Trudeau's smartest appointments was to name David MacNaughton, a consultant and lead Ontario political organizer for Trudeau, as his ambassador to Washington. MacNaughton and Freeland's office designed a massive, continent-wide program of constant contact between Canadian officials at multiple levels and absolutely anyone in the US who could be made aware of the value of the bilateral trading relationship. The Canadians included every federal cabinet minister, but also provincial premiers, big-city mayors, figures from every party—Saskatchewan premier Brad Wall, Harper's interim successor Rona Ambrose, and others. Their travel itineraries took them to every corner of the US. They dropped in on members of Congress, state governors, chambers of commerce, local TV stations. The effort lasted for two years. It generated a pro-Canada lobby the likes of which America had never seen. I sometimes wonder what would have happened if Trudeau had picked five other big intractable problems and applied the same level of ingenuity and concentrated effort to them. At least he picked one.

But to reduce Trump to NAFTA would understate the way his election shook Trudeau. His election inflicted a cultural trauma on the Liberals. Trump was the opposite of a feminist. He thought climate change was a hoax. He had an odd fondness for dictators in North Korea, Syria, and elsewhere. In many areas, he was a chaos agent, a faintly ridiculous random-event generator, but on one file that was key to Trudeau's values—and Katie Telford's—he was relentless: he set the stage for the Supreme Court to overturn the *Roe v. Wade* abortion-rights decision by applying a strict pro-life litmus test to his Supreme Court appointees. And to Canadian Liberals who viewed themselves as natural allies of progressive Democrats, the way Trump ended Hillary Rodham Clinton's political career felt much too personal.

The Liberals started seeing little Trumps everywhere. Provincial Liberal governments in Ontario and Quebec went down to historic defeats in 2018 with the lowest share of the popular vote either party had ever won. Out went Kathleen Wynne and Philippe Couillard; in their place were Doug Ford and François Legault, perfect louts in Trudeau's eyes. In Alberta, Trudeau's relations with NDP premier Rachel Notley had been tense, but at least they agreed on climate policy. In 2019, Notley lost to Jason Kenney, an old Trudeau nemesis from the Harper days who was on the record calling Trudeau an "empty trust-fund millionaire" with "the political depth of a finger bowl."

Trudeau entered active politics in an age when the post-Cold War consensus in favor of multilateralism, collective action, free trade, and loosely patrolled borders was occasionally under fire but still relatively intact. A central assumption of his political rhetoric from 2012 to 2015 was that the Canadian government would find friends everywhere it went: the United States, Europe, China, Alberta. Now a new generation of flinty men had risen, not just to question the old consensus, but to disdain it with impunity.

This was the Liberals' mood in the spring of 2018 when they gathered in Halifax for another national convention. Clinton was finished, Couillard and Wynne would be soon, and while the SNC-Lavalin fiasco was still almost a year away, already Trudeau's re-election seemed less of a sure thing. A highlight of the convention was an onstage conversation between Gerald Butts and David Axelrod, the architect of Barack Obama's two winning presidential campaigns.

The pairing was catnip for Liberals, who like to believe they are doing the Democrats' work out here in the colonies. For much of the session, the two men reminisced about progressive policy victories—Obamacare, the Canada Child Benefit—and spoke with real feeling about the burden politics puts on families and personal relationships. But more than Butts, Axelrod brought urgent counsel for a progressive government that, unlike Hillary Clinton, hadn't yet lost: suit up for battle. "There are dark forces in our politics now, and sometimes they arrive in stealthy ways," Axelrod said. "You have to be prepared to push back."

Trudeau was still proud of his 2015 decision to campaign without attack ads. Now, Butts was asking the visiting strategist: what, after all, is an attack ad? Axelrod said it was perfectly fine for governments seeking re-election to tell voters about the cost of voting for the other side. "That's not to say that politics of destruction are the way to go," he said. But it would have been "derelict for us in 2012 not to make sure that people understood what the choices were."

Justin Trudeau watched the exchange between Butts and Axelrod from the front row of the Halifax conference hall. The American had brought a precious gift: permission. Obama ran the first time on hope, the second time on contrast. Trudeau would do the same. "I do not engage in personal attacks, but I will be very, very sharp on distinctions around policy," he said sixteen months later at Rideau Hall when he launched the 2019 campaign.

Two successive ethics commissioners had found Trudeau in violation of the conflict-of-interest act that Stephen Harper had passed in 2006. He had abandoned his electoral-reform project, bought a pipeline, kicked two of his strongest women cabinet ministers out of the Liberal caucus. His vacation on the Aga Khan's private island and his interminable family trip to India, which saw the Trudeaus repeatedly dressing in outfits most adult professionals in India don't wear to work, made people start to wonder whether he was simply a flake. He had legalized cannabis and doctor-assisted dying, brought in some sturdy social policy, underperformed consistently as a debater and public speaker. He was a mixed bag.

His main opponent was Andrew Scheer, a forty-year-old near-unknown who had been speaker of the House of Commons and, therefore, forbidden from stating his opinions for most of the time he'd been in Parliament. Scheer had needed thirteen rounds of automated ballot counting to defeat his main opponent, Maxime Bernier, for the Conservative leadership. Bernier left to form his own party and set about working as hard as he could to split the right-of-Liberal vote. So Scheer had only a shaky mandate to lead his party and a tenuous grasp on the broader Conservative electorate.

The Liberal campaign war room set about turning Scheer's candidate slate into a liability by reposting embarrassing old tweets from Conservative candidates. Then, in the campaign's second week, an astonishing thing happened. *Time* reported that as a teacher at Vancouver's exclusive West Point Grey Academy in 2001, Trudeau showed up for an "Arabian Nights" gala wearing dark makeup over his face and hands. *Time* published a photo. It was ludicrous. Within a day, two more photos from other incidents appeared: once when he was in junior college, another from his McGill University years. All told, Trudeau had spent perhaps fifteen years keeping dark makeup handy for social occasions.

After the news hit, the prime minister of Canada walked to the back of his campaign plane and apologized to the news cameras. "I shouldn't have done that. I should have known better and I didn't. I'm really sorry." He apologized again the next day in Winnipeg. "Darkening your face, regardless of the context of the circumstances is always unacceptable because of the racist history of blackface," he said.

And then . . . nothing happened. The polls were unsteady for a few days. Nanos measured a big increase in the number of respondents who "weren't sure" or "didn't know" how they'd vote. Then they were sure again and the Liberals and Conservatives were essentially tied. That's how they ended the election, with Scheer's Conservatives beating Trudeau's Liberals by 1.2 percentage points in the national popular vote and the Liberals winning thirty-six more seats than the Conservatives.

Trudeau had won re-election. In some ways, that's all that ever matters. He had made it through scandal and self-inflicted humiliation to win a second term. Little of his dignity or early promise survived the fight, but he was still standing. Scheer, in contrast, announced his resignation as Conservative leader seven weeks later.

PART THREE

Trudeau ran in 2015 on a promise to give the middle ground back to Canadians. By 2019, there was less middle ground. It had already been shrinking for years when he became the Liberal leader. He didn't cause the polarization of Canadian politics, but he noticed it, acted on it, and nudged it along. By 2021, that polarization came not only to save his career, but to define it.

Since 1965, teams of political scientists have surveyed thousands of Canadians after every federal election. Most of the questions don't change from one survey to the next, so the Canadian Election Study has become a basic tool for measuring Canadians' attitudes towards politics, the economy, and one another over time. It's now older than the latest generation of academics who run it.

One of the Canadian Election Study's standard sets of questions is the "feeling thermometer." Respondents are given the name of a political party and asked how they feel about it on a scale from 0 to 100. A score of zero represents "a very negative feeling" and 100 represents a "very positive feeling."

Respondents usually give a higher score to the party that receives their vote than to the parties competing against it, which only makes sense. From 1988 to 2004, the average gap between the two scores, for supporters of all parties, was about twenty points. It would bump up or down a bit from election to election, but it stayed close to twenty points from the 1988 rematch of Brian Mulroney's Progressive Conservatives and John Turner's Liberals to 2004, which was the first election for Paul Martin, Stephen Harper, and Jack Layton as leaders of their parties.

Then the gap started to widen, fairly consistently through five consecutive elections, until in 2019 it had more than doubled to forty-four points.

In 1988, most respondents gave marks between thirty and sixty out of a hundred to the opposing party, which we can take to mean Liberals or New Democrats for Conservative voters, and Conservatives (or the old Progressive Conservative, Reform, and Canadian Alliance parties) for Liberal or NDP supporters. This indicates they rated the other side near the middle of the scale. By 2019, scores between zero and ten were almost seven times more common than in 1988, making that bottom-of-the-barrel grade the most common response. Canadians used to think the parties they voted against were all right, just not their cup of tea. Lately, they more often believe the opposing party is beyond redemption.

There is a term for this: "affective polarization," partisan disdain for the other side. This gap is actually bigger than partisans' real disagreement on the issues facing government, such as taxation, immigration, or crime and punishment. It hasn't only been happening in Canada. Affective polarization was first identified in the United States and, like most things, it's bigger there than here. But investigators have also found affective polarization increasing over the last few decades in Switzerland, France, Denmark, and New Zealand.

One of the academics studying polarization in Canada is Eric Merkley at the University of Toronto. He's measured "considerable hostility" in Canadians' views of opposing parties—the Conservatives for Liberal and NDP supporters, and the Liberals (more than the NDP) for Conservatives. In one of Merkley's surveys, 65 percent of respondents believed the word "selfish" applied to supporters of the opposing party and 70 percent said "hypocritical" applies. What about when you feed them kinder words? How about "open-minded?" Well, no, 68 percent reject that as a word to describe the opposing party.

Some of the perceived gap is attributable to self-perception and to genuine disagreement on issues. Merkley found that NDP and Liberal supporters are likelier to self-identify as being on the left than they used to, with Conservatives placing themselves more emphatically on the right. He also found the two camps' answers on policy questions have been diverging over time. In the 1990s, Liberals were close to Conservatives on support for immigration, same-sex marriage, or how they would rank jobs and environmental protection if forced to choose. Now, Liberals' opinions on all those issues are closer to New Democrats than to Conservatives.

But partisans' ideas about their opponents actually exceed real differences. "Canadians think they are more polarized than they actually are," Merkley writes. How many Liberals or New Democrats are LGBTQ? Respondents overestimate by fifteen points more than when they're asked the same question about Conservatives. How many Conservatives are fully vaccinated for COVID-19? Here respondents guess low, missing by fifteen points more than when they guess for other national parties.

Affective polarization erodes communities because people who support opposing parties increasingly don't even want to know one another. In the United States, about 40 percent of respondents say they'd be upset if their son or daughter married someone from another party, or if such a person became their neighbor. In Canada the number is lower—Merkley found it at 29 percent—but that's higher than if the new in-law was from another race, francophone, atheist, or queer. It's about the same as the level of unease with a Muslim neighbor or in-law.

What causes an increase in affective polarization? Partly it's that political parties have become more homogeneous, a phenomenon political scientists call "sorting." Political parties used to be broad coalitions. Now each is more monolithic in its members' perceptions.

Political scientists say polarization is partly elite-driven. That matches what I've seen. The old notion that "at the end of the day, we're all working for Canadians" is not the sort of thing you hear in Ottawa these days. Soon after he became prime minister, Harper put the word out among Conservative staffers to stop drinking in bars frequented by Liberals. In 2017, a senior Trudeau advisor came to speak at a *Maclean's* event where Garnett Genuis, a pro-life Conservative from an Edmonton riding, won the magazine's "Parliamentarian of the Year" award. The award winner was selected by other parliamentarians, and the winner's name was always a surprise. "I had to stay because I was part of the program," the Trudeau advisor told me, "but I saw a lot of our people leave when Garnett got the prize and I'm proud of them."

I'd add party funding as a driver of polarization. Jean Chrétien and Harper ended the old system, where businesses and labor unions could give very large donations to their preferred party. In 2011, Harper also ended the per-vote subsidy that gave every established party a periodic windfall from the government. Now every party's main source of donations is individual Canadians, whose total annual donation is capped at $1,700. To succeed, parties need to separate their supporters from their money, a few dollars at a time, by constantly telling horror stories about what will happen if the other side gets in.

A final, powerful driver of polarization, once it begins to dominate the political culture, is events. In the years before and since Trudeau came to power, the news headlines from home and abroad provided no shortage of horrors for partisans to interpret by their increasingly disparate lights.

In 2008, the US banking system started to collapse. Two successive presidential administrations, George W. Bush's and Barack Obama's, bailed out the banks to the tune of hundreds of billions of dollars. Individual homeowners were not so fortunate. A Great Recession produced untold pain and hardship in America's old industrial heartland. Chronic unemployment and unsafe work conditions produced a continent-wide market for an ever-deadlier opioid spiral—OxyContin, then heroin, increasingly adulterated with fentanyl. Firearms, alcohol, and suicide completed the mounting slaughter. In 2014, the US reached an astonishing milestone: life expectancy peaked at 78.9 years, and then started to decline for the first time since the First World War.

The sense of unprecedented alienation from the old elites that were supposed to take care of people—government, finance, industry— drove two virulent new protest movements in America: the Tea Party on the right and Occupy Wall Street on the left. Flip sides of the same devalued coin, both movements were convinced the leadership class was ransacking the country and that ordinary people had to take direct action to stop it.

In Kentucky, Ben McGrath covered a Tea Party rally in 2010 for the *New Yorker*. He found the protesters "suspicious of decadent élites and concerned about a central government whose ambitions had grown unmanageably large . . . Large assemblies of like-minded people, even profoundly anxious people anticipating the imminent death of empire, have an unmistakable allure: festive despair."

Kurt Andersen wrote the cover ode to *Time's* 2011 Person of the Year, "The Protester." It was the moment of the Arab Spring revolutions in the Arab world and North Africa. "All over the world," Andersen wrote, "the protesters of 2011 share a belief that their countries' political systems and economies have grown dysfunctional and corrupt—sham democracies rigged to favor the rich and powerful and prevent significant change."

A Canadian echo of Occupy was the Idle No More protests for Indigenous rights, which closed roads, railways, and bridges across the country in 2012. The terrorist attacks on Parliament Hill and at Saint-Jean-sur-Richelieu in 2014, the global surge of migrants from Syria and elsewhere into Europe in 2015, the Yellow Vest populist protests in France in 2018, the copycat United We Roll convoy into Ottawa in 2019—all of them contributed to a feeling that ordinary people and their supposed leaders had lost control of events.

Polarized politics don't make it impossible for votes to swing, but they do make it harder. Voter allegiances become stickier. Partisans become likelier to put up with excesses or outrages on their side because they imagine the other side would be far worse. We saw some of this in the reaction to the humiliating revelation of Trudeau's blackface history.

When times get really weird, viewers turn to their trusted news sources for context. On Radio-Canada's French-language, 24-hour news channel RDI, that means *24•60*, the nightly context-and-interview show hosted since 2008 by Anne-Marie Dussault. The night after the Trudeau blackface story broke, Dussault's lead guest was Dany Laferrière, one of Quebec's most important novelists. Black, born in Haiti, he had worked and lived in Montreal for decades. His novels, in the original French and often in translation, have earned him a worldwide audience. He is the first Quebecer, the first Canadian, and the first person born in Haiti to be elected to France's Académie française by its members.

Dussault asked Laferrière what he made of the photos.

"It's astonishing," Laferrière replied from home. "It literally pushed me to my library to find the three magnificent volumes of the *One Thousand and One Nights.*" He held the three paperback volumes up for the camera. Few people looking at the bizarre old photos had paid much attention to the fact that the West Point Grey photo took place at an Arabian Nights theme party. For Laferrière, that detail was key.

"There's always a context. That's why literature exists. It's existed for a very long time. It can help us understand what people do, what's going on behind the scenes. Sometimes even the people in the middle of events don't always understand.

"For instance, we're talking about blackface, brownface, which is mostly about American culture, American politics," he continued.

"The very history of Blacks and Whites in America, and of slavery. But Aladdin is something different. Aladdin doesn't refer to a living being. He's a literary figure who comes from the *One Thousand and One Nights*. Aladdin is a story that comes from Persia. And these days we know very well that Iran—which is to say, Persia—is in a complex and complicated situation with the United States. For us in Canada, Persia arrives in a situation absolutely out of the *One Thousand and One Nights*. Which means Canada is a fairly pacifist country. We're in the domain of literature, whereas the United States may not be far from being at war."

Dussault reminded Laferrière that Trudeau had apologized twice in two days for his behavior. Was Laferrière saying that the photos didn't even fit the definition of blackface?

"Oh no, it's certainly not blackface," Laferrière said amiably. "You know, with blackface, you absolutely have to have the goal of ridiculing and de-humanizing the other. And in the first image I saw, where he was accompanied by magnificent young women, and he had a really nice turban, the women didn't seem frightened by his presence."

Here RDI helpfully displayed the image in question on the screen. Sure enough, both Trudeau and the four young women in the photo were smiling. "Sometimes people want to be Black," Laferrière said. "Sometimes it's a fantasy—the fantasy of being somebody else."

Dussault pressed on. Did Laferrière accept Trudeau's apology? "I don't have to accept an apology from Mr. Trudeau. Mr. Trudeau's apologies have nothing to do with this story. They're just politics." And when he dressed up as Harry Belafonte and sang "The Banana

Boat Song" for a school assembly? Was that also an expression of admiration? "Yes, absolutely," Laferrière said. "He would like to be Harry Belafonte! And Harry Belafonte is Black too!" Sometimes that's just how far people go when they really admire somebody's work, he said. "I admire Jorge Luis Borges," he added. Which was a bit of a non sequitur because Borges is Argentinian, and Laferrière wasn't wearing whiteface as he spoke.

I'm not sure I've ever heard something as ridiculous as Laferrière's analysis in my life. The producers of the main Radio-Canada network, however, judged Laferrière's analysis so helpful that they ran a long excerpt on the main network's flagship national newscast, *Le Téléjournal*, a few hours later.

Dany Laferrière isn't a Liberal militant. I'm sure he'd be as comfortable voting Bloc or NDP as Liberal. But by the second week of a close election campaign, he knew what he didn't want, and he knew what would happen if the Liberals stumbled. So he made his peace with a highly idiosyncratic interpretation of the available evidence. In their various ways, other voters did the same.

Having won his re-election, Trudeau kept sorting the electorate. Since the thing that had saved him—far more than his patchy record or his inconstant character—was the feeling that a change in vote from Liberal to Conservative must not be contemplated, he set out to make the distinction even clearer. The latest round of political protests provided a handy opportunity.

In March 2020, COVID-19 would obliterate every other preoccupation in Canadian public life, but in February it seemed Trudeau's greatest test was a nationwide cascade of road and rail blockades by Wet'suwet'en, Mohawk, and other activists against

TC Energy's Coastal GasLink pipeline in British Columbia. New Democrats and most Liberals supported the protesters strongly. Conservatives found the protests outrageous. Businesses affected by the blockades became more worried the longer they continued.

By February 18, the protests were endangering the country's food supply. Trudeau told the House of Commons the moment was grave. "Young, old, Indigenous, and newcomers are asking themselves what is happening in this country," said the prime minister. People could sense that "these protests are serious and that this is a critical moment for our country and for our future."

Serious how? Characteristically, Trudeau was imprecise.

"This is about things that matter," he said.

Which things?

"Rights, livelihoods, the rule of law, and our democracy."

How do they matter?

"Indigenous rights, climate action, law and order, and building a clean economy are things we will not achieve by degrading our democracy."

Did he have a better idea?

"It is past time for this situation to be resolved," he said.

Great. By whom? He didn't say.

"Patience may be in short supply," he added, "and that makes it more valuable than ever."

Andrew Scheer was still leader of the Conservatives. Following his election defeat, he had been forced by his caucus to announce his resignation and the party was preparing to select a new leader. In the meantime, he was in the House of Commons and apparently believed he was participating in a debate. He rose to call Trudeau's remarks a "word salad" and "the weakest response to a national crisis in Canadian history."

The part Trudeau had left out, Scheer said, was "a clear denunciation that the actions of these radical activists are illegal." A "mob" was "trampling over the legal system which has governed our country for more than 150 years."

Scheer's bellicose speech definitely contrasted with the other leaders' remarks. "It's inspiring to see the youth rising," the NDP's Jagmeet Singh said cheerfully.

But Trudeau decided Scheer had done much more than define one end of the debate. Scheer "disqualified himself from constructive discussions with his unacceptable speech," Trudeau told reporters later that day. Singh told reporters Scheer's remarks were racist.

Nor was Trudeau content to castigate the Opposition Leader. He shunned him. The prime minister convened Singh, Elizabeth May of the Green Party, and Yves-François Blanchet of the Bloc Québécois to a meeting in his office to discuss the blockades. Scheer was the only party leader he didn't invite, even though Scheer led the largest caucus and his party had just won a plurality of the popular vote.

That was on a Tuesday.

On the following Friday, Trudeau appeared before reporters with the usual cabaret line of nodding cabinet ministers to swallow himself whole. Perhaps the mounting pressure from businesses had made him reconsider. "The barricades must now come down," he said. "The injunctions must be obeyed and the law must be upheld." In substance, his stance was now difficult to distinguish from Scheer's. And he had closed the distance in record time.

It was a dizzying sequence of events, but Trudeau had nevertheless managed to send a clear signal that there was acceptable and unacceptable debate in Canada; that he would decide which was which; and that the Conservatives, who had won 220,000 more votes than the Liberals in the 2019 election, could be disqualified from public discourse when he pleased.

And then the world shut down.

Three weeks after Trudeau called for the Coastal GasLink blockades to end, a virus from China infected Sophie and caused the prime minister to cancel a scheduled meeting with provincial premiers in Ottawa. Much of the global economy shut down as everyone who could stay home from work did. The lockdown continued, with only sporadic breaks, for almost two years.

There's a lot to be said about Trudeau's handling of the COVID-19 pandemic. I said much of it in an earlier instalment of Sutherland Quarterly, *An Emergency in Ottawa*. I think the government was culpably slow to take the virus seriously as a domestic threat, but Canada was hardly the only country where that happened. Trudeau's government moved with increasing assurance to isolate Canadians and keep them safe until vaccines became available. It could do this, to a greater extent than most Western governments, because it was in better fiscal shape. That's because the four prime ministers before Trudeau—Mulroney, Chrétien, Martin, and Harper—took the country's fiscal health more seriously than he would have in their place. As a result, Canada could pay more people to stay home without working, and more businesses to stay open without customers, than could other countries, and fewer people died here.

In the early mad scramble for vaccine doses, people who didn't want an injection were not a problem. Later, they were viewed as a public-health menace by people who thought that, at some sufficiently elevated vaccination rate, the virus could be eliminated from Canadians' lives. Those opinions mapped fairly neatly along party lines, so Trudeau decided on the eve of the 2021 election to turn vaccine reluctance to his advantage by making the election a referendum on vaccine mandates. The Freedom Convoy was the result.

Still, taken across the whole two years, the Trudeau government has a reasonably good story to tell about its handling of the pandemic. Somebody who worked closely with Trudeau once told me he gets the big things right and everything else wrong. His examples of "big things" were saving NAFTA and surviving COVID.

For our purposes today, what's most striking is that, throughout the period between the lockdown and vaccine abundance, partisan sorting continued. Two of its casualties were Scheer's successor and Trudeau's finance minister.

One of the biggest surprises of my career was the unmistakable hint of euphoria in the way some Liberals spoke in the early days of the lockdown. The economy was in free fall. Thousands were dying. Nobody knew how long it would last. And at the progressive end of the spectrum, some people were saying, *here's our chance.*

I heard it over the phone when I checked in with a Liberal political staffer of my acquaintance a few weeks into the crisis. "It's not every day you get a job to completely redefine the role of government for a new era," said my friend. "This is a once-in-a-lifetime opportunity."

There was something going around, and it wasn't COVID-19. In mid-May, Hélène Buzzetti wrote in *Le Devoir* about a similar conversation. "It'll be a good time to be a progressive government," an unidentified senior Liberal said. "There are a lot of us who are dreaming big, who have an audacious vision for this enormous social and economic challenge before us."

Another source told her: "I know that behind the scenes, this thinking is underway and I have more confidence than ever, because Justin Trudeau seems to really grasp the immensity of the moment, how important it is for his political legacy, and we'll have a plan that will be exciting to put to Canadians at the next election."

This was a bizarre way to think about a chaos bomb on the scale of a global pandemic, but apparently some people couldn't help themselves. In late March, only days after the coronavirus lockdown began, Michael Sabia published a remarkable opinion article in the *Globe and Mail*.

Sabia is a public servant and business executive who stepped down at the end of 2019 as head of the Caisse de dépôt et placement du Quebec, the province's public-sector pension fund. In the *Globe*, he wrote that keeping Canadians safe and solvent was small potatoes compared to the real work ahead. The big challenge would be building the new post-lockdown economy. "Governments will need to lead on this," Sabia wrote. "Leaving it to chance will only make the reignition process longer, more difficult, and more haphazard. What's more, we would forfeit a precious opportunity to shape our future economy. Remember Rahm Emanuel's famous: 'You never want a serious crisis to go to waste.'"

To this day I find the chutzpah astonishing. People were afraid to go to grocery stores. Sabia wanted the government to "begin thinking now" about "a new generation of infrastructure" and "spending on education. About clean tech and retooling our health-care system. And about refinancing for the long term a small and medium enterprise sector that will emerge from this crisis battered but still the engine of jobs in our economy."

Two weeks after Sabia's op-ed appeared, Trudeau made him the chair of the board of the Canada Infrastructure Bank, a $35-billion fund Trudeau launched in 2018 as leverage to attract an even larger sum of foreign investment. It has never worked. But that wouldn't be Sabia's problem for long. By the end of that first COVID year, Sabia was the government's new deputy minister of finance. The job was open because the incumbent deputy minister had quit, and he'd quit because, in August, Trudeau's office leaked embarrassing stories about the minister, Bill Morneau, until Morneau quit.

To Trudeau, this was excellent news. He gave Morneau's old job to Chrystia Freeland. After her swearing in, Trudeau was still in the grip of his inexplicable euphoria over a global catastrophe. He said to reporters, "We can choose to embrace bold new solutions to the challenges we face and refuse to be held back by old ways of thinking. As much as this pandemic is an unexpected challenge, it is also an unprecedented opportunity."

In a world of partisan sorting, it only makes sense that even as Trudeau was turning his government upside down in anticipation of the coming green paradise of progressive triumph, his opponents accused him of using COVID-19 as a pretext to hand the country over to foreign interests.

In June 2020, the World Economic Forum, an international NGO that runs an annual retreat for the important and self-important at Davos, Switzerland, started pushing out absurd COVID-19 techno-triumphalism in bulk. The WEF's preferred label for this sort of thinking was "The Great Reset." It had a Great Reset page on its website, where it published stuff like this: "To achieve a better outcome, the world must act jointly and swiftly to revamp all aspects of our societies and economies, from education to social contracts and working conditions. Every country, from the United States to China, must participate, and every industry, from oil and gas to tech, must be transformed. In short, we need a 'Great Reset' of capitalism."

Trudeau was hardly unaware of this line of argument. Indeed, he put real effort into mimicking it. In September, he told a United Nations conference by video call: "This pandemic has provided an opportunity for a reset. This is our chance to accelerate our pre-pandemic efforts to reimagine economic systems."

Two months after Trudeau made that video, Conservative MP Pierre Poilievre posted a petition on his website urging people to help him "Stop the Great Reset." This scheme "would re-engineer economies and societies to empower the elites at the expense of the people," the petition's text said. "Canadians must fight back against global elites preying on the fears and desperation of people to impose their power grab." The petition gathered more than 80,000 signatures within days, which would ensure the signatories continued to receive emails on similar topics. Elite polarization.

A lot of the news coverage at the time wondered where Poilievre got such crazy ideas. The answer is that he got them from Davos and Trudeau, and added some topspin of his own. Freeland, who had received a battlefield promotion to replace a G7 finance minister at the height of a global fiscal crisis, was on the board of the WEF and remains there to this day. I have never seen her explain why it's worth her time or, since she has a full-time job, why it's worth ours. People who think the WEF is nefarious never stop mentioning its connection to Freeland. I don't think the WEF is nefarious, but I think it's easier to convince yourself there's something wrong with it when the top Canadian in its org chart won't talk about it.

At some point, the spirit of solidarity that united Canadians against a virus was bound to fray. This made election timing tricky. Premiers with minority governments in New Brunswick and British Columbia called transparently opportunistic snap elections at the end of 2020 and were rewarded with majorities. Trudeau called his own election at the earliest moment he could decently do so, at the end of the summer of 2021, two years after the last. Unfortunately, Afghanistan chose that same week to collapse in a heap of futility, creating an urgent refugee crisis in a corner of the world where Canada had almost no resources.

Voters respond to opportunistic elections in different ways, depending on the circumstances. Usually, they don't mind voting whenever they're asked. But they can get ornery when reminded by events that there's pressing business a government is leaving behind as it goes fishing for a bigger mandate. That's what happened to Jean Chrétien in 1997, when flooding on the Red River in Manitoba made his early election call look callous. The result wasn't terrible for the Liberals, but that election ended with the weakest of Chrétien's three majority mandates.

Now Trudeau was going to the polls as Afghanistan burned. The complicated logistics of extracting from chaos those Afghans who had helped Canadian troops and journalists looked like full-time work for a serious government. Trudeau couldn't explain why he was walking away from it. By the campaign's second week, the Liberals' sturdy polling advantage had melted away.

Affective polarization was Trudeau's salvation. In the days before the election call, he had made a big change in his approach to COVID-19 vaccinations. For months, he'd been reluctant to impose any kind of obligation on people to get a jab. But in the late innings of the pandemic, whether to get vaccinated was no longer a mere difference of opinion. It was turning into a cultural divide, with far more voters in favor of vaccine mandates than opposed to them. By toughening his stance, Trudeau could appeal to that majority and back the Conservatives into a corner. Days before the election call, he announced his government would require vaccination on flights, trains, and in federally regulated workplaces if re-elected.

At the same time, Trudeau's main opponent was trying to appeal to a nearly vanished middle ground. Erin O'Toole had learned a genteel, centrist brand of Conservatism in Ontario and Nova Scotia. In the party's 2020 leadership race, he ran to the right of the contest's biggest name, former foreign affairs minister Peter MacKay, with appeals to Christian Conservatives and to the resource sector, including a promise to scrap Trudeau's carbon tax. But once the leader's job was his, O'Toole moved back to the center, where he was most comfortable. He even had a carbon tax plan, although he refused to call it a carbon tax. It was a lot of zigging and zagging for one man to do in a short span of time. It produced a lot of uncertainty, both in his own party and with the electorate at large.

On COVID-19, O'Toole wanted to permit people who took rapid tests to work and travel even if they weren't vaccinated. It was essentially Trudeau's position from a few months earlier, but the Liberals now ran against it as reckless and life-threatening.

Putting vaccines, the most emotional issue of the moment, at the heart of their campaign probably saved the Liberals from further collapse. After all, a lot of people supported the strongest possible measures against the pandemic. Of course, many of those opposed to the measures were furious. Some started showing up at Trudeau campaign events, waving flags and shouting insults, both at Trudeau and at people who showed up to hear him. Trudeau had to cancel a campaign event at Bolton, northwest of Toronto, for security concerns.

Yet the Liberals kept pushing. They made O'Toole abandon his own platform language on gun control, and tormented him for days over an old promise to favor private-sector "innovation" in health care. You could buy a hip replacement in Montreal before the campaign, and you can still buy one there today, but the Liberals have always believed that only Liberals should be trusted to run two-tier health care.

In the end, voters sent the parties back to a Parliament that had barely changed from before the election. The Liberals' share of the popular vote dipped to 32.62 percent, the lowest of any victorious party since Confederation, but they managed to pick up five seats on close races. The NDP gained one seat, the Conservatives and Bloc Québécois none at all. O'Toole had watched Trudeau tack to the left and hoped to move into the centrist territory the Liberals had abandoned. But that's not really how it works these days. All O'Toole had really managed to do was make his party doubt that he should be its leader.

At the end of January, thousands of truckers and assorted other malcontents converged on Ottawa from across the country. The Conservative caucus, largely rural, Christian, and fed up with COVID-19 restrictions, saw the Freedom Convoy as innocuous, if not heroic. Many of them greeted the protesters on their way to and from Parliament, brought them coffee and snacks. O'Toole couldn't decide how to respond. His MPs scheduled a vote on his leadership. "It's time for a reckoning," O'Toole wrote on Twitter. "To settle this in caucus. Right here. Right now. Once and for all. Anger vs. Optimism. That is the choice in simple terms."

O'Toole sounded pretty angry in the tweet, as people on Twitter often did, but in this instance he was casting himself as the voice of optimism.

Optimism lost.

Trudeau wasn't content to see the back of a third consecutive Conservative leader. His play for a return to majority government had failed. And the people who'd tried to disrupt so many of his campaign rallies had followed him back to Ottawa and set up camp on Parliament's front porch. Trudeau dusted off the never-used Emergencies Act to bring the Freedom Convoy to a belated end. He next set about securing an effective parliamentary majority to make up for the majority the voters had declined to give him.

On March 22, Trudeau and Jagmeet Singh announced a "supply and confidence agreement" by which the NDP would not vote to bring down the government until June 2025. In return, the Liberals agreed to implement a list of policies favored by the NDP, including subsidized dental care and universal pharmacare. The effect of the deal was to ensure the Liberals had four more years in power.

There is something about Trudeau that can spot an easy mark. In 2012, he knew the bankrupt and beaten Liberals would not refuse him a rule change that would turn their leadership selection process into a pure popularity contest. Now, a decade later, his attention turned to the bankrupt and beaten NDP. The supply-and-confidence deal gave Trudeau the stable hold on power that he craved. In return, the New Democrats would be spared the quick election they feared.

Anyone taking a long view would have been struck by the distance Trudeau had traveled. He won his first election with a promise to ensure nobody would ever again win all the power with only a fraction of the vote. He won his third with the lowest share of the popular vote of any governing party in Canada's history, less than one vote in three. Now he had all the power anyway.

Of course some people would be furious. How was that his problem? They were rooting for the wrong side.

PART FOUR

Part of the way I'm wired as a political writer is that I tend to give winners the benefit of the doubt, for all their failings. This business is about what you do after you win, or it isn't about much. People called Jean Chrétien a fool while they spent decades losing to him. People said Stephen Harper was way outside the mainstream of Canadian politics while support for his party grew in three consecutive elections. I figure maybe the ones who keep winning know a thing or two about politics.

Justin Trudeau has defeated three different Conservative leaders. He could have lost any of those elections. He entered his first campaign in third place with a tiny caucus. Before and during his second campaign he gave Canadians excellent reasons to vote against him. The third time, he taped a sign saying OPPORTUNIST to his forehead on his way to Rideau Hall. He kept winning anyway. In June, he'll have had this job longer than Louis St. Laurent did. Nobody can take that away from him.

What are his qualities? I've spent less time talking to him than I had spent with Harper before he became prime minister, but politics in Canada is a village. Paths cross. I've seen him up close. On the afternoon of that *Maclean's* leaders' debate in 2015, I was running around the CityTV building in Toronto trying to find the makeup room when I bumped into Trudeau and a few of his advisors. "How are you doing?" he asked.

"I'm great, thanks," I said. "I've got the easiest job in that studio tonight."

"No, Paul, you've seen some of that stuff out there. I know you feel it."

My fitness to steal the national leaders' debate away from proper broadcasters was a matter of considerable debate on Twitter. A lot of people were sure I was the wrong person for the job because I'd written two books about Stephen Harper and was, therefore, impossible to trust, at least by Trudeau's admirers. (Somebody in his entourage, in fact, had peddled that argument to reporters around Ottawa while they tried to decide whether to accept a debate invitation they didn't want.)

I told Trudeau that as soon as he and Mulcair and Harper started talking, nobody watching would pay any attention to me. That was the end of our short chat. Off he went, advisors in tow. But what a strange moment it had been. Perceptive, emotionally direct. He'd shown real concern for me, or seemed to, amid everything that was going on in his own week. Probably it was part of a briefing note, or somebody had mentioned it to him at the front of the campaign plane. Doesn't matter. He still knew how to use it to make a connection.

Trudeau can be as callous as anyone, and more so than most. He kicked every senator out of the Liberal caucus after several of them gave their lives to the party. He dumped Marc Garneau, Omar Alghabra, Mona Fortier, and David Lametti from cabinet with no better reason than convenience. Once an Indigenous woman showed up at a fundraiser to complain about mercury poisoning. Trudeau watched the event security staff hustle her to the nearest exit, then said he was thankful for the donation she'd paid to get into the room. I mean, mercury poisoning. Holy Lord.

But he has also often shown remarkable self-awareness. I ran into him at a Montreal function in 2004 when he'd just started hosting a weekly radio show on CKAC, a French-language talk radio station. "I've been in Vancouver," he said. "I need to work on my French. This way I can [speak French] under pressure." That was the moment I knew he was getting ready for a political career. Working on his French in public, where he'd be highly motivated to improve because everyone could hear him screw up, was a quick way to become more electable as he prepared to run in a Quebec riding.

When I interviewed him for a *Maclean's* cover story in 2012, he explained in detail why the various kinds of people who got excited when he showed up in a room might not make a sturdy voter coalition. He sees his weaknesses clearly.

He is an introvert who has become skilled at pretending the contrary. After a rally where he seems to hunger for attention and human contact, he sometimes needs time alone, in a quiet room, playing video games on an iPad or doing nothing at all. I'm told his need to decompress at the end of his work day didn't always make him popular at home.

I often meet people whose job puts them into meetings with Trudeau. Diplomats, public servants, people from other levels of government, sometimes from other countries. I ask how they found him. The reviews are universally positive. He prepares. He grasps complexity. He can take criticism. You can blue-sky with him, imagine alternatives, play out various scenarios for how an issue might evolve. He has the thing that some politicians have, where he remembers the last time he saw you, even if it was under very different circumstances.

I trust the reviews. The people who say these things are not partisans. They'd have nothing to lose if they said he's a buffoon who's lucky he hasn't choked on his own tongue. But politics isn't just conversation, it's management. The challenge for a political leader is to build a system that amplifies his qualities and mitigates his shortcomings. Trudeau's governments amplify both.

He's been making a good first impression for as long as he's been alive. He's athletic and charming. His last name has helped more often than not. Skeptics often find he's more impressive in person than they expected. So he's built his political career on first impressions. When he threw open the doors to the Liberal leadership process, he was tilting the process in favor of superficial interest and away from thoughtful consideration. When he brought out a cabinet that was half women, or skipped the first day of the 2015 campaign to march in Vancouver's Pride parade, or hosted Ban Ki-Moon in the biggest ballroom in the National Capital Region, he was finding new ways to say: *here I am, somebody fresh in a stale game.*

In his first year in power, he tried hard to turn others' excitement at his presence into hard economic advantage for Canada. It was probably worth a try. At Davos in January 2016, he met Mary Barra from General Motors, Jim Smith from Thomson Reuters, and Satya Nadella from Microsoft. At the annual conference in Sun Valley, Idaho, six months later, he met Mark Zuckerberg, Jeff Bezos, and

Tim Cook. Each time, Trudeau made a pitch: *there are great things happening in Canada, let's talk.*

At the end of that first year, he hosted some of the world's biggest institutional investors at Toronto's swank Shangri-La Hotel to pitch Canada as an investment destination. The Hong Kong Monetary Authority. Norway's Norges Bank. The Olayan Group from Saudi Arabia. Singapore's Temasek Holdings. The Qatar Investment Authority. Sweden's Länsförsäkringar group of insurance companies. The deepest pockets in the world. At the front of the room, Trudeau, nine of his cabinet ministers, and a slide deck the government had developed in cooperation with BlackRock, the $9-trillion New York investment bank. Working on a slide deck with BlackRock probably bent some rule somewhere, but Trudeau wanted to make sure he was talking to these people in a language they understood.

Very little of it had any lasting effect. None of the institutional investors at the Shangri-La has ever invested in a Canada Infrastructure Bank project, and none seem to have changed their investment posture with regard to Canada. Basically, Trudeau and a third of his cabinet bought them lunch. "Overall, global FDI inflows and outflows mostly followed the same pattern as Canadian FDI inflows and outflows, so Canadian trends are largely in line with international trends," Global Affairs Canada wrote in its State of Trade 2023 report. In other words, Canada didn't become a different place because Justin Trudeau had some meetings.

After the optimism of 2016, Trudeau's handshaking expeditions in 2017 and 2018 became more hectic and nervous. In opposition, he saw China as a sort of wall socket that Canada could plug into for all its economic growth needs. "What if our goal was to become Asia's designer and builder of livable cities?" he wrote in the *Financial Post* in 2012. (The answer, it turned out, was that Asia would build its own.) John McCallum, Trudeau's new ambassador to Beijing, arrived there at the beginning of 2017 as the emissary of that ambition. "My slogan is more, more, more," McCallum told the *Toronto Star.* "We want to do more trade, more investment, more tourists."

I think Trudeau was astonished when Beijing didn't buy what he was selling, or would only do so on Xi Jinping's terms. As trade talks became stuck, Trudeau flew to Beijing at the end of 2017 on short notice, with hardly any formal agenda. It was another attempt to use his presence to change minds. He got nowhere. The Chinese side cancelled the closing news conference. That was the end of his trade talks with China. It was Trudeau's most frustrating foreign trip to that time, although he topped it two months later when he visited India with his family. Since then, there have been fewer attempts to personify change by going to a trouble spot. Indeed, there has been a marked reluctance to put Trudeau into a situation where he might come home empty-handed.

The cruelly limited payoff from such meet-and-greets with pluto-crats began a reversal in Trudeau's attitude toward private business. At first, he hoped big companies would put money into Canada. Later, it became Canada's job to put money into big companies.

In the early going, if you were a CEO from a tech firm, Trudeau saw you as an emissary from a prosperous green future and therefore as an excellent partner. The best example is the 2017 announcement by Google's Sidewalk Labs subsidiary that it would lead the development of Waterfront Toronto, a prototype for an IT-driven city of the future. Sidewalk planned to spend $1.3 billion on the project, which would trigger $38 billion in private investment by 2040. Trudeau showed up for the announcement and told the crowd that he and Eric Schmidt, the executive chairman of Google's parent company, Alphabet, "have been talking about collaborating on this for a few years now." Which he probably shouldn't have said, because Waterfront was supposed to be running a competitive bidding process.

More important, in 2020, the whole thing collapsed amid privacy concerns about the data Sidewalk would have collected. Trudeau had put a lot of his own time, hope, and reputation into a project that didn't pan out. Contrast this outcome with the government's stunning 2018 purchase of Kinder Morgan's Trans Mountain pipeline for $4.5 billion. Sure, the cost of completing the pipeline has since multiplied sevenfold, and it will be damned interesting to see whether the feds can ever find a buyer. But at least the government owns a pipeline.

Over time, the Trudeau government has actually come to prefer this sort of arrangement. It has developed a frosty relationship with businesses that can succeed on their own. It prefers to deal with businesses that would fail if the government didn't keep bailing them out. A company that doesn't need the government is unpredictable. It might say things Trudeau wouldn't. It might simply be unimpressed, as the executives of Shopify have been, even after the government gave its young and telegenic founders positions on boards and panels in the early years. A private company might leave the country altogether, as Encana did in 2019, or support a different political party.

Companies that would fail if some federal contract or subsidy were withheld are much more reliable. They never stop being grateful. They say the sort of things a government wants companies to say. Sometimes the lines blur so thoroughly that it's hard to tell where the company stops and the government begins. In 2019, Postmedia reporter David Pugliese sent questions about the welding on new Arctic patrol ships to the federal departments of national defence and public services. Ninety minutes later, he got a call from the president of Irving Shipbuilding. The Trudeau government's relationship with the economy has become an elaborate network of codependency.

* * *

Trudeau's changing relationship with private enterprise is one of a few ways he's adjusted while settling into power for the long haul. I've mentioned how he moved to the left in response to the changing partisan landscape, the expectations of his activist voter and donor base, and global events. His management style has changed, too. Or rather, after a few months, his management style settled into a characteristic pattern he seems disinclined, or unable, to change further.

There are two ways to manage over the long haul. One is to be managerial. The other is to defy the long haul by trying eternally to recapture the excitement of your first victory. Justin Trudeau is the second type.

Just about anyone can make a list of Canada's intractable problems. Low wages. Low skills. Low business investment. Rudimentary public infrastructure. Fitful engagement with the rest of the world, distant as it is from our isolated shores. A resulting tendency to promise the world more than Canadians usually feel like delivering.

Every once in a while, even this government acknowledges that problems like this exist. There was a startling paragraph in Chrystia Freeland's 2022 budget, starkly different from the forced optimism of so many government pronouncements: "Most Canadian businesses have not invested at the same rate as their U.S. counterparts. Unless this changes, the OECD projects that Canada will have the lowest per capita GDP growth [from 2020 to 2060] among its member countries." That's a problem worth spending a decade to fix.

You might come up with a different list of problems. But whatever was on our lists, fixing the items on them would require similar approaches. Rewards for effort would be limited at first. Attempts to move big, stubborn dials would have to be incremental and sustained for a long time. Policies to address entrenched problems would probably have to be iterative: try something, see whether it helps, tweak what works a bit, discard what doesn't work at all, and repeat. Iteration requires humility, because it means admitting, frequently, that the last thing didn't work.

There's a word for the slow, terribly public work of working through a big problem in public and being honest about the results. That word is "deliverology." It's become a joke in Ottawa among the few people who remember it, but I always thought there was something to the idea. So did Trudeau, early on, although it's since become his road less traveled.

For a few weeks at the beginning of 2016, word spread that Trudeau's man, Gerald Butts, admired the work of a public servant named Sir Michael Barber in Tony Blair's UK government. Barber called his approach "deliverology." It was simply the act of frequently updating citizens on progress against measurable and known goals.

What matters in this mindset is the result. Your plan for getting there is not particularly important, because you'll probably have to adjust or discard it based on how your efforts affect progress. "Get started, learn fast from the real world, understand the messy reality, and adjust the plan accordingly," Barber wrote in one of his books.

One of the few areas where Trudeau has done something like this is in eliminating long-term boil-water advisories in Indigenous communities. In 2015, there were 105 communities where, for a year or longer, residents had to boil water before drinking it. Trudeau promised there'd be zero by 2021. In 2021, there were still fifty-two such communities. It's terribly frustrating work. As soon as a remedy is applied in one place, the water becomes unsafe somewhere else. As I write, the number still stands at twenty-six.

I think this is one of the projects Trudeau should be proudest of. An intractable problem is smaller than it was because the government didn't give up, even when results were discouraging. None of his predecessors even tried. Do you suppose his successor will?

But what did it take? Patience, focus, thick skin, and constant disappointment in return for almost no political credit. The alternative to all of that hassle is to just keep announcing stuff, as though the announcements themselves were the point. This is the second model for government over the long term, and it is the model Trudeau has preferred. Its appeal is easy to see.

First, it creates endless little simulacra of the excitement that greeted the arrival of a new government in 2015. There's a podium, there's a microphone, there's an invited crowd, there are one or more cabinet ministers nodding in the background. The PM or one of his ministers makes an announcement, the bigger the better, and, at that moment, nobody can yet be certain that it will all turn to grief.

We're going to build a magic bank that will attract four dollars from the rest of the world for every dollar the government spends. We're going to diversify trade away from Donald Trump's America, so Canadian companies can hawk their wares in less annoying countries. We're going to plant two billion trees. We're going to use the size of Canada's government to drive innovation by setting aside $65 million a year to buy new Canadian tech for use inside the government. Our navy will become a big player in the Indo-Pacific. We're going to give $2,000 vouchers for four-night camping trips to 75,000 less-privileged children and their families. We're going to send 28,000 young Canadians into mom-and-pop businesses to help them grow online, turning every shop on Main Street into the Canadian-headquartered global champions of tomorrow. We're going to save democracy in this dark and worried world by building a Canadian Centre for Peace, Order and Good Government.

These were all things Trudeau promised. Some of them happened, kind of. The Canada Infrastructure Bank exists. But even by its own optimistic analysis, it has attracted one investor dollar, not four, for every government dollar.

The late Jim Carr was Canada's first minister of trade diversification. He was also its last. His job title amounted to an assertion that Canada could just skip right past its biggest traditional export market. The hard truth, as reported by the Canadian government's own Trade Commissioner Service, is that the United States is almost always the first export market for Canadian companies that later do business in other countries. So the best way to promote diversified trade is to encourage companies to trade first in the United States. Apparently, somebody in the government decided this was too hard to explain to voters, even though I just explained it in a tweet. When the message had finally sunk in, the government stopped claiming it would diversify trade.

A few reporters in Ottawa have done good business for years by checking past Trudeau promises to see whether they panned out. The camping vouchers appeared in the 2019 platform and were never heard from again. The Peace, Order and Good Government Centre appeared in the 2019 platform and the 2021 platform. Trudeau made it his main promise at Joe Biden's first Democracy Summit at the end of 2021. Global Affairs launched a working group in 2022 to design the democracy center. The working group disbanded in mid-2023. There's still no democracy center.

Sometimes, to avoid embarrassing stories, the government makes it harder for ordinary people to check its homework. There used to be a website where you could track the progress on boil-water advisories. A couple of years ago, the line graph that showed progress since 2015 disappeared. You can still see the total number of advisories. You just can't see what the number used to be, unless you've been grabbing screenshots.

From 2007 to 2015, from Stephen Harper's second year in office until Trudeau's first, Canada had a Science, Technology and Innovation Council with a simple mandate: track Canada's science performance against that of other countries. The STIC Council, made up of university presidents, business leaders, and top-ranking civil servants, published a report every two years on Canada's relative science performance. Basically, the news was always bad, so in 2015 the Trudeau government published the last STIC report, which was worse than the three before it. Then Trudeau's government shut down STIC. Now there are no more embarrassing reports about Canada's science performance, although the data is out there and if you put it in a report, it would still be embarrassing.

In 2021, the government announced it would use "the best available data" and follow "global best practices" to produce Canada's first National Infrastructure Assessment, a "forward-looking road map out to 2050." The idea is that it is unwise to spend tens of billions of dollars without knowing what you need. The idea is correct, which is why it's strange to start making a road map after you've been in power and spending on infrastructure for six years. What's stranger is that the government has announced no progress towards even beginning its assessment in over two years. These things are not impossible to do. The UK produced a national infrastructure assessment in 2018 and another in 2023.

I know I'm pretty deep into the weeds here. I've written an essay that begins when Justin Trudeau was popular and ends while he's unpopular. I don't want to give the impression that I think it's because Canadians are furious at the end of STIC or the stillborn National Infrastructure Assessment. But if you multiply these examples across dozens of cases in other fields, it starts to look like a syndrome. Trudeau has built a government that can't stop announcing bright new days, even though it seems increasingly unable to deliver.

I think people feel this. I think it helps explain the deep decline in Liberal voter support after the summer of 2023, even though the apparent precipitating event, a pointless cabinet shuffle much like earlier pointless cabinet shuffles, seems far too small a provocation for such a large reaction. I don't think people blame Trudeau for doing a specific terrible thing last summer. I think people simply gave up on seeing a new, improved Trudeau government.

Some of this is a problem with systems Trudeau inherited and has not repaired. The federal public service, hundreds of thousands of salaried bureaucrats, is terribly demoralized. The bureaucracy used to generate ideas for new government projects. But since political parties started arriving in government with detailed lists of promises, public servants are mostly reduced to implementing plans they didn't generate. Bureaucrats used to exercise a robust challenge function. But in a polarized environment, their political masters are less likely to view resistance as thoughtful than as disloyal.

As the pertinence of the public service has declined, the Trudeau government has spent ever-growing amounts on outside consulting firms, especially McKinsey and Deloitte. Radio-Canada reported last year that the Trudeau government has paid McKinsey thirty times as much as the Harper government did. Consultants are smart people, but they're generally not around when their proposals are implemented. Accountability is a problem.

If the federal government's machinery is in terrible shape, so is this government's ability to work with other levels of government. This is a very Trudeau problem. He doesn't have a background in dealmaking, which requires reconciling conflicting interests in pursuit of a large goal. His patience for any process that requires give-and-take is sharply limited. That's why he went shopping for a permanent accord with the NDP as soon as he realized he'd stuck himself with a second minority Parliament. He made a big deal to avoid having to make endless little deals. It's also why executive federalism in this country, the quaint label for government by federal-provincial conference, with a prime minister and premiers making a deal and then letting their respective governments figure out how to implement it, is basically a dead letter.

At the end of 2018, Trudeau played host to the premiers in Montreal for a first ministers' meeting on—well, I was there and I have strong memories of the thing, but I had to go look up the news release to remind myself what it was supposed to be about. The release says they met "to discuss economic growth and jobs for Canadians." And it turns out they were in favor!

For anyone who's read about the bare-knuckle federal-provincial meetings of the 1960s through the early 2000s, the Montreal meeting was bizarre. Governments used to meet to argue about the details of a proposed accord. Or a constitutional amendment or a funding formula. The stakes were terribly high, because if somebody walked out of the meeting, it would collapse in public disarray. This Montreal meeting was a genuine innovation because nobody had anything specific to talk about. There was no offer from Ottawa, no demand from the provinces. The communiqué reads like angel food cake. "First Ministers agreed to lead a discussion on the development of a framework for a clean electric future," it reads in part. Of course, nobody stormed out. What, precisely, would they have been leaving?

I earned myself an exceedingly rare critical email from Trudeau's inner circle with the column I wrote after the Montreal meeting. This sentence in particular made Trudeau's staff sad: "What's missing in Justin Trudeau's version of executive federalism is an executive in the federal chair."

When I wrote that, I was channeling a remarkable paragraph from the ethics commissioner's report on the Trudeau family's trip to the Aga Khan's tropical resort. Mary Dawson was the commissioner. She questioned Trudeau and his advisors on his work style in general. They argued that it did not matter if Trudeau had some face time with his benefactor, the Aga Khan, because nobody should attach much significance to any meeting Trudeau ever had with anybody.

"The meetings he attends as Prime Minister are not business meetings," Dawson wrote that she had been told. "Rather, they are high-level meetings centered on relationship building and ensuring that all parties are moving forward together. Specific issues or details are worked out before, subsequently or independently of any meeting he attends."

Before, subsequently, or independently. If Trudeau meets you, a decision might be made before your meeting. It might be made later. It might even be made somewhere else while you're meeting. But you will not see the prime minister of Canada make a decision while you are meeting him.

The most recent federal-provincial gathering, on health care at the beginning of 2023, was a case of the decision being made before the meeting. The provinces wanted a lot of money. Trudeau wanted to give them less, but he had ideas for ways the provinces could run their health-care systems. He called the premiers to Ottawa. When they arrived, he gave them copies of their agreement. And that was the end of the discussion. They could take the money he was offering or they would get none. They could accept his conditions or go home with empty pockets. Fortunately for the premiers, the conditions were laughably general. Trudeau said they'd get $25 billion over ten years for "family health services; health workers and backlogs; mental health and substance use; and a modernized health system." Is there a province that isn't spending money on any of those things?

* * *

To sum up, Trudeau came to office with an ambitious agenda. As he promised at the US ambassador's Kentucky Derby party in 2015, it really was easy to dispel the notion that he had no ideas. What turned out to be hard was implementing the ideas. Rich people were disinclined to give Canada money. Parliament was more frustrating than he ever imagined. The premiers were all right as long as they had names like Couillard and Wynne, but the next generation were annoying and Trudeau didn't want them to watch him make decisions. Meanwhile, Donald Trump, COVID-19, and a war in Europe happened.

Over time, Trudeau, increasingly, has focused on the thing a federal government finds easiest and does best: send cheques.

Distributing cheques (and the corollary, administering tax benefits) has always been a key federal competence. Most other things are tricky. Provinces run hospitals and schools. Ottawa doesn't directly deliver many services. When it tries—borders—passports—evacuating people from distant trouble spots—it often has difficulty. Sending people cheques is a lower-risk enterprise. It also offers clear electoral advantages. Usually, the recipient of the money is pleased to get it. And if there's a chance that the cheques will stop coming if the Liberals lose power, the recipient will have a personal stake in the Liberals' re-election.

Not that sending cheques is problem-free. It terribly distorts priorities, both for the people who get the cheque and for anyone who doesn't. I've seen this in my own field of journalism. The Trudeau government has become ever more willing to subsidize news production, mostly through targeted tax measures, even though you won't find a line about that in their 2015 platform. The scale of the assistance, a whopping $30,000 per eligible journalist, swamps anything a qualifying news organization might do to improve its bottom line through purely journalistic decisions. Cover this fire or not? Put another reporter at City Hall? These decisions have far less impact on year-end financial results than the need to qualify for next year's government benefit. Which means, in the new world of deep subsidy, newsroom managers aren't primarily journalists any more. They're grant farmers.

Multiply that situation across all the aids and benefits for companies operating in some field the government thinks is important or, better, "innovative." In 2017, Kevin Page, the former parliamentary budget officer, and his colleagues at the University of Ottawa's Institute of Fiscal Studies and Democracy found that Ottawa was already spending almost $23 billion a year on 147 different programs to encourage skills development, innovation, and technology adoption in Canadian businesses. That's the infernal mess Trudeau inherited from generations of previous governments. He didn't make the mess. He's just made it worse, throwing layer after layer of new programs onto the pile: a Canada Digital Adoption Program, a Canada Growth Fund, a Global Hypergrowth Project, and more.

I've heard from businesses that have to spend more time applying for all this stuff than actually adopting new technology and work processes. The innovation subsidies thus make it harder to innovate. I've heard from others who have dealt with these programs for years. They know each new program forces the business to do things it wouldn't have chosen to do on its own, and distracts from a clear-eyed evaluation of the business's real interests. That's for all the businesses that decide to play the incentive game. The ones that don't are shut off from huge funding opportunities, simply because they preferred to make their own decisions. Will they make innovative decisions? It depends. If you have a few million dollars and you'd like to help build the green economy of tomorrow, it's not going to be terribly motivating to watch Ottawa buy a battery factory for $30 billion.

We are near the end of our story, and none of the stuff I've discussed in this chapter would automatically disqualify an incumbent government. Governing is hard work, harder since the pandemic, punishingly hard in an era of global political chaos. It's not necessarily fatal for a government to make empty promises or to retreat into a silo that other levels of government can't penetrate or to make a swamp where the most productive part of the economy was supposed to reside.

It would be possible to imagine Trudeau coming back yet again if he had lately shown any inclination toward introspection or humility, or a driving urge to improve his game. In the absence of those qualities, bad habits become entrenched.

In his memoir, Trudeau writes that at the 2012 Mont Tremblant leadership planning retreat, he told his friends that the Harper government's "basic flaw" was its "inability to relate to or work with people who do not share its ideological predisposition. I said that Mr. Harper's extreme rigidity, his belief that disagreement and dissent are signs of weaknesses to be stamped out, would have a corrosive effect on Canadian public life over time." One must always take care not to become what one deplores.

Some Liberal readers will be frustrated that I've spent no time dwelling on the flaws of the prime minister's opponents, especially Pierre Poilievre, who'll be the fourth Conservative leader Trudeau faces in an election. They will say, *who could reason with that guy? Who could rise above a defensive crouch when he never stops attacking?* And especially: *how can any mundane criticism of Trudeau be fair, knowing what kind of government would replace him?*

I'm familiar with the argument. It was Trudeau's re-election pitch in 2019 and 2021. It's what Liberals are already saying about 2025. It might yet work one more time. A lot of people expect the pretty boy to get beaten up, but they expected that before and they were wrong then.

But here's the thing about a polarized political environment: it's not the other side that makes people lose faith in your project. Poilievre's had the same shtick since he was fourteen. Sometimes the Conservatives have won elections, sometimes they've lost. If people thought Trudeau was providing coherent government that understood the value of a buck, that he followed through on his promises and made serious changes in the event he screwed up, he'd have an easier time on defense. If voters think he's presiding over a shambles and that he thinks he and his favorite staffers have tenure, guilt-tripping voters won't help.

The question is whether you think polarization gives you a license or a burden. Do you say, "I get to be sloppy and presumptuous for years on end, because when the election comes I can ring a bell and scare my voter base into line?" Or do you say, "I promised to provide good government, not just fashionable opinions. I do not have the right to let my side down."

The boxing match was always a bad metaphor. Waiting for the other guy to wear himself out is a stance unworthy of a prime minister. I prefer something Trudeau said on the night he won his first election. He said Canadians want "a PM who never seeks to divide Canadians, but takes every single opportunity to bring us together. You want a prime minister who knows that if Canadians are to trust their government, their government needs to trust Canadians, a PM who understands that openness and transparency means better, smarter decisions."

We still do.

ABOUT THE AUTHOR

Paul Wells is one of Canada's most experienced political journalists. After many years at *Maclean's*, *National Post* and *The Gazette*, he now publishes a subscription newsletter at paulwells.substack.com. He is a frequent commentator on French-language and English-language radio and television, and is the author of *An Emergency in Ottawa*.

GIVE A <u>THOUGHTFUL</u> GIFT

1 YEAR PRINT & DIGITAL SUBSCRIPTION

SAVE 20% OFF THE $19.95 PER ISSUE COVER PRICE

- **Four** print books
- **Free** home delivery
- Plus **four** eBooks
- **Free** digital access to all SQ publications
- Automatic renewal

DELIVERY & PAYMENT DETAILS

Subscriber Info

NAME:
ADDRESS:
EMAIL: PHONE:

Payment Options

- Enclose a cheque or money order for $67.99 (includes HST) made out to Sutherland House Inc. Send to Sutherland House, 304-416 Moore Ave, Toronto, ON, Canada M4G 1C9
- Debit my Visa or MasterCard for $67.99 (includes HST)

CARD NUMBER: ____ ____ ____ ____   **CVV:** ___
EXPIRY DATE: __ / __   **AMOUNT:** $
PURCHASER'S NAME: **SIGNATURE:**

OR SUBSCRIBE ONLINE AT SUTHERLANDQUARTERLY.COM

GET THE <u>WHOLE</u> STORY

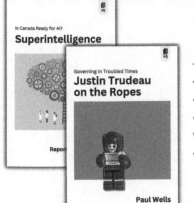